À BAS LES FRONTIÈRES! 1

Tony Mais, Alan Proffitt and Helen Silverstone

John Murray

A Bas Les Frontières!
Students' Book 1 ISBN 0-7195-4913-2
Teaching and Assessment Resource Book 1 ISBN 0-7195-4914-0
Cassette Pack 1 ISBN 0-7195-4915-9
Students' Book 2 ISBN 0-7195-4916-7
Teaching and Assessment Resource Book 2 ISBN 0-7195-4917-5
Cassette Pack 2 ISBN 0-7195-4918-3

© Tony Mais, Alan Proffitt and Helen Silverstone 1991

First published 1991
by John Murray (Publishers) Ltd
50 Albemarle Street,
London W1X 4BD

British Library Cataloguing in Publication Data
Mais, Tony
  A bas les frontieres.
  Students' bk. 1
  1. French language. Usage
  I. Title II. Proffitt, Alan III. Silverstone, Helen
  448
  ISBN 0-7195-4913-2

Designed and produced by The Pen & Ink Book Company Ltd

Cover photograph courtesy of Images Colour Library

Printed by Mateu Cromo Artes Graficas, Spain

For copyright ownership of photographs and non-original material see p.157

CONTENTS

INTRODUCTION

A Bas Les Frontières is a course for young people who have or want to see a practical reason for learning French in the later years of school or in Further Education, and who want to have useful skills at the end of their course of study.

French has usually been taught either purely for academic achievement or because it was assumed that the learner would go to France on holiday. As the frontiers come down in the European Community, many people from Britain may have the opportunity to work in France and, perhaps more importantly, a knowledge of French will be required in many jobs in this country, either for dealing in person with French people who come here, or on the telephone or by letter.

A Bas les Frontières presents a series of practical work-based situations in which you can practise the language and skills you are learning. This aims to provide a language survival kit for a range of jobs here or in France where some knowledge of French is required, or a basis for further vocationally related language study.

We hope you enjoy this course. Being able to talk to people in their own language is not only a useful skill in the world of work but is also exciting on a social level. We hope you will feel actively inspired to seek situations where you can use your French skills or to include language options in your further training.

Bonne chance!

1 PREMIÈRE PARTIE

Le Travail en Famille

In this section, you go to Toulouse to live and work with a family called Djamil. The things you learn could be used anywhere when dealing with French children, or when working in a French household.

UNITÉ 1

On se présente

Before setting out for Toulouse, you and the Djamil family exchange some basic information about yourselves.

At the end of this unit you should be able to:

1 Tell someone your name, including spelling it in French.
2 Say where you live.
3 Say how old you are.
4 Say what you like doing.
5 Ask someone about themselves.

Un peu de lecture

Une demande de travail en famille

The Agence Hubert is arranging the work placements. Your teacher will give you an application form for you to fill in, giving your personal details. Here is a similar form which your friend Cathy has just filled in.

Agence Emploi Hubert

tél: 57.13.13.31.

6 Impasse de la Garderie
33100 Toulouse

Demande de travail comme...... *Au pair* ....

Nom...... *Dawson* ....

Prénoms...... *Cathy* ....

Adresse...... *15 Guildford Place,*
Edinburgh 5 ....

Age...... *15* ....

Signature...... *Cathy Dawson* ...... Date *le 2 février, 1991*

Ecoute la cassette (1)

Je m'appelle Yousef

You have received some photos and a cassette from the Djamil family. Match up the names on the tape to the photos to see if you can work out who is who.

1

2

3

4

5

6

Sais-tu dire bonjour?

Salut!

Ça va?

Bonjour

Ça va bien merci, et toi/vous?

Et maintenant à toi

Ecoute la cassette (2)

Ecoute la cassette (3)

Et maintenant à toi

Ecoute la cassette (4)

Comment t'appelles-tu?

1 Ask your partner's name and let him/her answer, then swap roles.
2 For extra practice, pretend to be a member of the Djamil family. Can your partner point to the right photo?

Encore les Djamil

Listen carefully as each member of the Djamil family spells their name, so you will know how it is written. Try to write out each name as it is spelt then check to see how you did.

L'alphabet en français

Listen very carefully to the alphabet in French — you will need to be able to spell English names for French people.

Comment ça s'écrit?

Tell your partner your name and then spell it in French. If you need extra practice on the alphabet first, listen to the tape again and then try to recite the alphabet with the tape.

Où habitent-ils?

To get to Toulouse you take a train from Paris. On it you meet a group of young French people. Listen as they tell you where they are from, and check each place on the map.

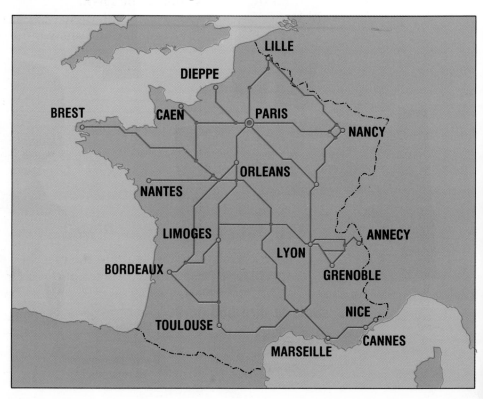

Now see if you can note down where each person lives. Do not write in this book!

Nom	Ville
Philippe	
Sophie	
Paul	
Albert	
Hélène	

Sais-tu dire où tu habites?

Où habites-tu?

J'habite une grande ville qui s'appelle . . .
J'habite un petit village près de . . .
J'habite à la campagne près de . . .

Où habitez-vous?

Nous habitons . . .

Et maintenant à toi

Où habites-tu?

1 Ask and answer the question with your partner.
2 Now pretend that you are both French and choose one of the places on the map as your home town.
3 Work with another pair and, pretending both you and your partner live in the same place, ask and answer the question: 'Où habitez-vous?'

Sais-tu compter?

1 un	6 six	11 onze	16 seize
2 deux	7 sept	12 douze	17 dix-sept
3 trois	8 huit	13 treize	18 dix-huit
4 quatre	9 neuf	14 quatorze	19 dix-neuf
5 cinq	10 dix	15 quinze	20 vingt

Ecoute la cassette (5)

Les âges des enfants Djamil

On the train you listen again to the cassette you received from Mme Djamil. Note down the ages of the children.

Franck _____ Nadia _____

Annie _____ Joseph _____

Ecoute la cassette (6)

Cinq jeunes se présentent

On the train to Toulouse you meet another group of French people. Make a copy of the following table and see if you can note down in your book some of their details.

Prénom	Nom	Domicile	Age

Sais-tu dire ton âge?

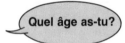 Quel âge as-tu?

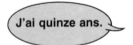 J'ai quinze ans.

Et maintenant à toi

Quel âge as-tu?

1 Ask your partner's age and make a note of it.
2 Now ask three other people their ages.

Sais-tu te présenter?

Je m'appelle..............................
Ça s'écrit ....
J'ai................................... ans.
J'habite ....

Sais-tu demander à un ami/ une amie?

Comment t'appelles-tu?
Comment ça s'écrit?
Quel âge as-tu?
Où habites-tu?

Et maintenant à toi

Présente-toi!

Here is an example of a French identity card.

Your teacher will hand out some cards to you and to your partner.
1 Acting as the person on your card, introduce yourself to your partner.
2 Now take a different pair of cards and ask your partner some questions to find out who he/she is, and his/her age and address.

Sais-tu demander les détails sur quelqu'un?

> Comment s'appelle-t-il?
> Ça s'ecrit comment?
> Quel âge a-t-il?
> Où habite-t-il?

Sais-tu présenter un ami/une amie?

> Il/elle s'appelle.....................................
> Ça s'écrit..
> Il/elle a .... ans.
> Il/elle habite ....

Travaillez en groupe

Faire des présentations

Introduce your partner to the rest of the group. They should greet him/her. When everyone in the group has introduced each other, move around the class making introductions. You could ask questions too.

Sais-tu dire ce que tu aimes?

> J'aime .....le football
> .....le shopping
> .....le golf
> .....le tennis
> .....la natation
> .....le cinéma
> .....la pêche
> .....les Beatles
> .....la musique pop
> .....la télé
> .....le disco
> .....les disques
> .....les jouets
> .....les enfants
> .....l'athlétisme
> .....sortir en voiture

. . . et poser la question?

> Qu'est-ce que tu aimes?
> vous aimez?

Ecoute la cassette (7)

La famille Djamil aime . . .

On the cassette you received are details of the family's interests. Make notes of what everyone likes doing.

Yousef ————————————
Françoise ————————————
Franck ————————————
Nadia ————————————
Annie ————————————
Joseph ————————————

Je me passionne pour le football

On the seat in the train you find a copy of the sports newspaper *L'Equipe*
Since one of your own favourite players was recently transferred to
Marseille you check to see who they are playing today. You also look to
see who Toulouse are playing, as Franck is a keen supporter.

12è journée

(12ᵉ journée)
Ce soir, 20 h 30

*MONACO (1) - Lille (9)
*NIORT (2) - Brest (16)
*PARIS-S-G (12) - Saint-Étienne (3)
*BORDEAUX (4) - Laval (17)
*MONTPELLIER (8) - Nantes (5)
*LENS (20) - METZ (6)
*TOULOUSE (14) - Matra Racing (7)
*CANNES (13) - TOULON (10)
*MARSEILLE (11) - Auxerre (19)
*LE HAVRE (18) - NICE (15)

You find the league table in the paper. Work out, for both Marseille
and Toulouse:
1 Where they are in the league.
2 How many games they have won, lost or drawn.
3 How many goals they have scored and what their goal differences are.
4 Work out which team in the league has scored the most goals.
5 Which team has conceded the most goals.

Pts = points
J. = joué (*played*)
G. = gagné (*won*)
N. = nul (*drawn*)
P. = perdu (*lost*)
p. = pour (*goals scored*)
c. = contre (*goals conceded*)
Diff. = différence (*goal difference*)

Classement

	Pts	J.	G.	N.	P.	p.	c.	Diff.
1. MONACO	16	11	7	2	2	20	9	+ 11
2. Niort	13	11	6	1	4	13	11	+ 2
3. St-Étienne	13	11	5	3	3	17	19	— 2
4. Bordeaux	12	11	4	4	3	16	13	+ 3
5. Nantes	12	11	4	4	3	14	11	+ 3
6. Metz	12	11	5	2	4	12	9	+ 3
7. Matra RP	12	11	3	6	2	11	13	— 2
8. Montpellier	11	11	3	3	4	16	13	+ 3
9. Lille	11	11	4	3	4	14	11	+ 3
10. Toulon	11	11	3	5	3	10	8	+ 2
11. Marseille	11	11	4	3	4	15	16	— 1
12. Paris-SG	11	11	5	1	5	12	13	— 1
13. Cannes	11	11	3	5	3	11	15	— 4
14. Toulouse	11	11	5	1	5	11	16	— 5
15. Nice	10	11	5	0	6	13	17	— 4
16. Brest	9	11	5	3	3	13	10	+ 3
17. Laval	9	11	3	3	5	12	11	+ 1
18. Le Havre	9	11	2	5	4	12	16	— 4
19. Auxerre	8	11	2	4	5	7	11	— 4
20. Lens	8	11	3	2	6	11	18	— 7

Et maintenant à toi

A vous tous

Un peu de lecture

Prends ton stylo

Qu'est-ce que tu aimes?

The young people you meet on the train want to know about your likes, and you ask them about their interests too. Work with your partner and then swap around within your group.

Trouve le double

Your teacher will give you a card. You have to find the person with the same card as you. Do this by asking questions in French.

La lettre de Franck

While you were still in England, Franck Djamil wrote to you to tell you about himself. Note down details about him from the information in his letter.

> Salut! Je me présente : je m'appelle Franck Djamil et j'ai seize ans. J'habite à Toulouse – c'est une grande ville dans le sud de la France – Nous sommes quatre enfants! mes deux soeurs s'appellent Nadia et Annie et mon petit frère s'appelle Joseph. Il a quatre ans. J'ai une amie qui s'appelle Florence – voici sa photo. Elle est jolie, n'est-ce pas? Qu'est-ce que tu aimes faire? Moi j'aime le sport. J'aime le rugby, mais je me passionne pour le football. L'équipe toulousaine s'appelle le TFC – Tu aimes le sport aussi? J'aime aussi la musique moderne et les discos.
>
> Amitiés
> Franck

Tes détails

1 Note down on a card your personal details: name, age, home town, interests.
2 As the basis of a letter about yourself, give your personal details. Here are some words to help you start:

Je m' ....

J' .... ans

J' .... à ....

J'aime ....

3 Now note the same details about your partner:
Il/elle s'.............. ....

Vocabulaire

adresse (*f*)	address	**natation** (*f*)	swimming
âge (*m*)	age	**nom** (*m*)	surname
aimer	to like, love	**où**	where
athlétisme (*m*)	athletics	**prénom** (*m*)	first name
bonjour	good morning, good day, hello	**pêche** (*f*)	fishing
		quel, quelle	what
ça va?	everything OK?	**s'appeler**	to be called (name)
carte d'identité (*f*)	identity card	**salut!**	hello, hi!
comment	how	**sœur** (*f*)	sister
disque (*m*)	record	**sortir**	to go out
domicile (*m*)	home, where you live	**sud** (*m*)	south
enfant (*m/f*)	child	**toi**	you (to one person whom you know well or a child)
équipe (*f*)	team		
frère (*m*)	brother	**trouver**	to find
habiter	to live in	**voiture** (*f*)	car
jouet (*m*)	toy	**vous**	you (to several people or one person whom you don't know well, an older person)
lettre (*f*)	letter		
maintenant	now		
merci	thank you		

UNITÉ 2

La famille

Arriving in Toulouse, you spend the first few days getting to know the Djamil children and some of their friends.

At the end of this unit you should be able to:

1 Introduce your family to someone.
2 Give a simple description.
3 Say what someone is wearing.
4 Say what colour something is.
5 Use polite forms when needed.

Ecoute la cassette (1)

Mme Djamil présente sa famille

When you arrive, Mme Djamil introduces you to her family. See if you can link the name to the word explaining each person's relationship to Mme Djamil.

Voici mon mari   Nadia
Voici ma fille   Joseph
Voici ma fille   Franck
Voici mon fils   Yousef
Voici mon fils   Annie

Sais-tu présenter ton collègue?

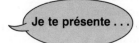
Je te présente . . .

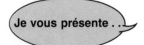
Je vous présente . . .

Et maintenant à toi

Présente ton collègue

1 Introduce your partner to your teacher.
2 Introduce your partner to another friend.
3 Introduce your partner to a group of people.
Don't forget that the person who is introduced must shake hands and say hello.

Sais-tu présenter ta famille?

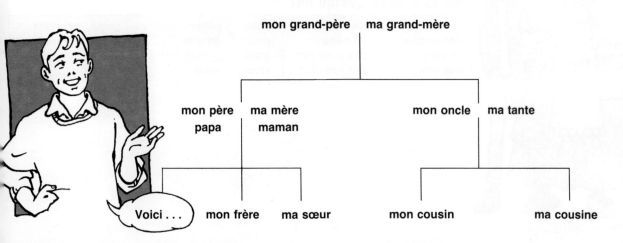

mon grand-père   ma grand-mère

mon père   ma mère   mon oncle   ma tante
papa   maman

Voici . . .   mon frère   ma sœur   mon cousin   ma cousine

Et maintenant à toi

Présente ta famille

Using a photo of your family or some drawings you have prepared, tell the Djamils about your family. Work with your partner. You can make up a family if you wish.

Sais-tu présenter la famille d'une autre personne?

Voici	sa grand-mère	son grand-père
	sa mère	son père
	sa sœur	son frère
	sa tante	son oncle

Et maintenant à toi

Présente la famille d'un/e ami(e)

Show someone else the pictures of your partner's family and explain who they are.

e.g. Voici la famille de Richard. Voici sa mère, etc.

Sais-tu compter jusqu'à soixante?

21 vingt et un	32 trente-deux	49 quarante-neuf
22 vingt-deux	33 trente-trois	50 cinquante
23 vingt-trois	39 trente-neuf	51 cinquante et un
29 vingt-neuf	40 quarante	52 cinquante-deux
30 trente	41 quarante et un	53 cinquante-trois
31 trente et un	42 quarante-deux	60 soixante

Prends ton stylo

Ta famille

Annie is writing an essay about you, the person who has come to help in the family. She wants some details of your family. Write down five or six sentences for her.

e.g. Mon père s'appelle David, il a trente-six ans.

Sais-tu décrire quelqu'un?

un homme	un enfant	petit,	petite	gentil,	gentille
une femme	un bébé	grand,	grande	jeune,	jeune
un garçon	des jumeaux	gros,	grosse	mince,	mince
une fille	des jumelles	vieux,	vieille		

Ecoute la cassette (2)

La famille de Florence

Franck has a girlfriend called Florence. Listen as she tells you about her family. Make some notes, using a table like the one below.

	Nom	Age	Description
Mon père	*Frédéric*	*43*	*grand*
Ma mère			
Mon frère			
Ma sœur			
Mon oncle			
Ma tante			
Mon grand-père			
Ma grand-mère			

Un peu de lecture

La lettre de Michel

Robert is on holiday with his family in Toulouse. He asks you to help him with a letter he has received from his new pen-friend Michel just before leaving home. Note down some details for him.

Le 10 juillet 1990

Cher Robert

J'ai reçu ton nom d'une agence de correspondance. J'espère que tu vas vouloir m'écrire.

Je m'appelle Michel Heuser et j'ai 15 ans, je suis grand et j'ai les cheveux blonds. J'habite 50, avenue des Lilas, à Strasbourg. Mon père s'appelle Michel aussi et lui aussi est grand. Je n'ai pas de mère mais ma grand-mère habite avec nous. Elle s'appelle Jeanne et elle est petite. J'ai un frère, Yvan, qui a 10 ans. Lui, il est plus petit que moi, mais grand quand même pour un garçon de 10 ans. Il a les cheveux bruns comme les avait maman.

Ecris-moi vite s'il te plaît et parle-moi de la famille

Michel

Prends ton stylo

La lettre de Robert

Robert wants to write back. Here are the details he gives you. Help him write the letter.

Name: Robert Smith
Age: 14
Home town: Bridlington
Appearance: Short

Father is 38 and is short too. His name is John.
Mother is 39 and is tall. Her name is Anne.
Has a sister called Jenny who is 16 and a brother called Daniel who is 10. Daniel is small but Jenny is tall, like her mother.

Sais-tu dire quand tu es né(e)?

> **Quand es-tu/est-il (elle) né(e)?**
> **Je suis né(e) le dix février.**
> **Mon anniversaire est le vingt-deux décembre.**
> **Son anniversaire est le deux avril.**
> **C'est aujourd'hui le premier juin.**

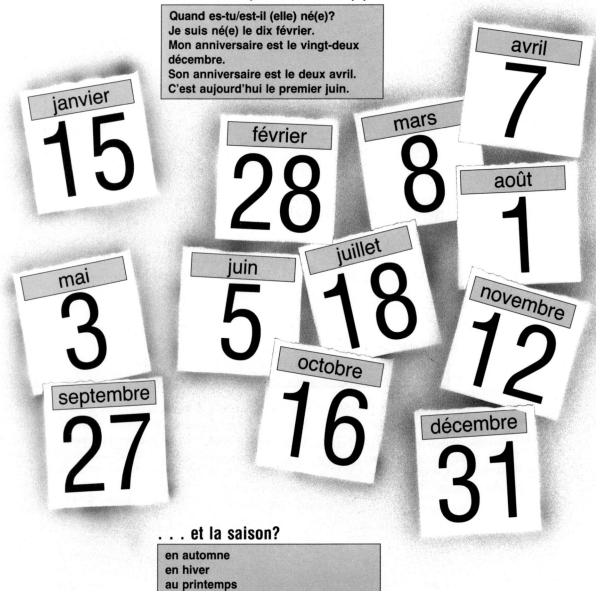

avril
7

janvier
15

février
28

mars
8

août
1

mai
3

juin
5

juillet
18

novembre
12

septembre
27

octobre
16

décembre
31

. . . et la saison?

> en automne
> en hiver
> au printemps
> en été

Ecoute la cassette (3)

Les anniversaires des enfants Djamil

Mme Djamil tells you when each of the children's birthdays are. Make a note of the dates to help you remember.

Franck ——————

Nadia ——————

Annie ——————

Joseph ——————

Et maintenant à toi

Décris ta famille

The Djamil children are curious to know about your family. Working with a partner, give as many details as you can.

You and your partner can ask each other questions about your family and friends.

Toi	Ton collègue
As-tu un frère ou une sœur?	J'ai un frère/ J'ai une sœur. *or* Je suis enfant unique.
Comment s'appelle ton frère?	Il s'appelle . . .
Il est grand/ petit/ gentil?	
Comment s'appelle sa sœur?	Elle s'appelle . . .
Elle est grande/ petite/ gentille?	
C'est quand son anniversaire?	

Now ask other people the same questions.

Sais-tu décrire les vêtements?   . . . et les couleurs?

un pantalon		bleu	bleue
une jupe		vert	verte
une chemise		gris	grise
des chaussures		noir	noire
des chaussettes		rouge	rouge
un chapeau		jaune	jaune
une veste		orange	orange
un tricot		blanc	blanche
une robe		long	longue
un pullover		court	courte

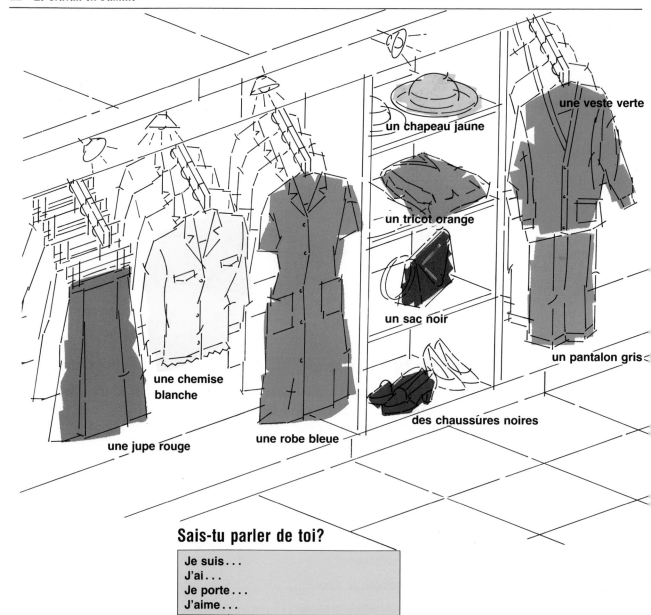

une veste verte

un chapeau jaune

un tricot orange

un sac noir

un pantalon gris

une chemise blanche

une jupe rouge

une robe bleue

des chaussures noires

Sais-tu parler de toi?

Je suis...
J'ai...
Je porte...
J'aime...

Et maintenant à toi

Je sors ce soir

You are going out this evening and Nadia wants to know what you will be wearing. Describe your outfit. Work with a partner, who should ask the question:

> Qu'est-ce que tu portes?

You might reply:

> Je porte une chemise bleue.

A vous tous

Loto de vêtements

You will be given a 'clothes bingo' card. As your teacher calls out the name of an article of clothing, mark it off on your card. When you have a 'full house', call out **'Loto!'**.

Les amis de Franck

Franck shows you some photos of his friends. Can you put a name to each photo?

1

2

3

4

5

Tu connais bien ton collègue?

Write out phrases to describe your partner using the following as a guide.

Il/elle s'appelle ....

Il/elle a .... frères.

Il/elle a .... sœurs.

Il/elle est fils/fille unique.

Il/elle est .... (grand, petit, gros, mince, gentil).
    (N.B. Elle est grande, petite, grosse, gentille.)

Il/elle porte ....

Il/elle aime...

Qui est-ce?

Joseph has a new model house and wants to begin collecting the animals who live in it. He asks you to draw a picture of the Bear family – **la famille Bonours** – who are described in the packaging of the model house.

Read the following descriptions and draw pictures to represent the bears being described.

'Maman Bonours est petite. Elle porte une jupe rouge et une chemise blanche, des chaussettes vertes et des chaussures jaunes.'

'Papa Bonours porte un pantalon noir et une chemise jaune. Il est gros. Il porte des chaussures grises.'

'Michelle Bonours a deux ans. Elle est très petite. Elle porte une petite robe blanche et des chaussettes rouges.'

'Grand-père' Bonours a cinquante-cinq ans. Il porte une veste grise, un pantalon orange et des chaussures noires.'

'Edouard Bonours est gentil. Il porte un pantalon jaune, des chaussures rouges et un anorak bleu.'

Les familles Sylvania™

Les amis de la forêt articulés, costumés et à collectionner.

TOMY®

Une lettre à un ami

After you have been in Toulouse a little while, you have a few days off. Since a pen-friend of yours lives quite near in Carcassonne, you decide to visit him. You will be met at the station by the mother of your pen-friend. Write to describe yourself and your clothes so that she will recognise you.

Vocabulaire

anniversaire (*m*)	birthday	**jupe** (*f*)	skirt
août	August	**long, longue**	long
aujourd'hui	today	**mai**	May
automne	autumn	**maman**	mum, mummy
avril	April	**mari** (*m*)	husband
blanc, blanche	white	**mars**	March
bleu, bleue	blue	**mince**	slim
bébé (*m/f*)	baby	**mon, ma, mes**	my
chapeau (*m*)	hat	**mère** (*f*)	mother
chaussettes (*f*)	socks	**noir, noire**	black
chaussures (*f*)	shoes	**novembre**	November
chemise (*f*)	shirt	**né, née**	born
court, courte	short	**octobre**	October
décembre	December	**oncle** (*m*)	uncle
enfant (*m/f*)	child	**orange**	orange
été	summer	**pantalon** (*m*)	trousers
femme (*f*)	wife, woman	**papa**	dad, daddy
fille (*f*)	daughter, girl	**petit, petite**	small, short
fils (*m*)	son	**porter**	to wear
frère (*m*)	brother	**premier, première**	first
février	February	**printemps**	spring
garçon (*m*)	boy	**pullover** (*m*)	sweater
gentil, gentille	nice	**père** (*m*)	father
grand-mère (*f*)	grandmother	**quand**	when
grand, grande	big, tall	**robe** (*f*)	dress
grand-père (*m*)	grandfather	**rouge**	red
gris, grise	grey	**septembre**	September
gros, grosse	big, fat	**sœur** (*f*)	sister
hiver	winter	**son, sa, ses**	his/her
homme (*m*)	man	**tante** (*f*)	aunt
janvier	January	**ton, ta, tes**	your
jaune	yellow	**tricot** (*m*)	sweater, cardigan
jeune	young	**vert, verte**	green
juillet	July	**veste** (*f*)	jacket
juin	June	**vieux, vieille**	old
jumeaux/jumelles	twins		

UNITÉ 3

Chez la famille

As you settle in with the family in Toulouse, you get to know the layout of the Djamils' flat and details of their household very well.

At the end of this unit you should be able to:

1 Give your address.
2 Describe your house in simple terms.
3 Describe your own and other rooms.
4 Understand spoken and written descriptions.
5 Talk about your pets.

Ecoute la cassette (1)

Les amis d'Annie

Annie's friends are saying where they live. Look at the map which gives certain code letters representing their addresses. Write down the friends' names, then beside each name note down the correct code letter.

1	Louise	
2	Jean-Luc	
3	Sophie	
4	Moïse	
5	Michel	

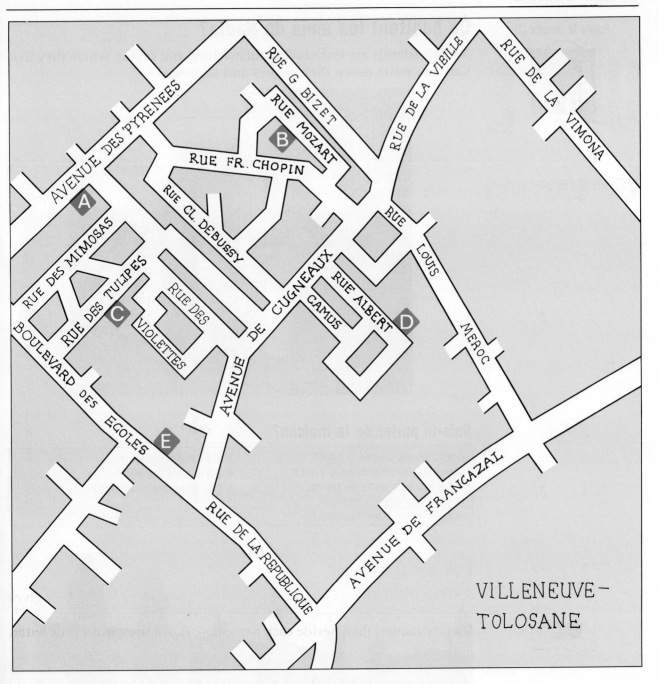

VILLENEUVE-
TOLOSANE

Et maintenant à toi

Quelle est ton adresse?

1 Say where you live in French.
   (Street names remain the same, whether said in English or French, for example: London Road = London Road, rue de Paris = rue de Paris.)
2 Ask your partner where he/she lives, and write down the answer.
3 Pretend you live in Villeneuve and choose a street from the map. Now answer the question: 'Quelle est ton adresse?'

Où habitent les amis de Nadia?

Nadia's friends are introducing themselves, and saying where they live. Can you write down their names and addresses?

Sais-tu parler de ta maison?

Combien de pièces y a-t-il?	Il y a neuf pièces.
Combien de chambres y a-t-il?	Il y a quatre chambres.
Il y a aussi la salle de bains,	Il y a une chambre d'hôte.
le salon, la salle à manger,	
la cuisine et le vestibule.	

Voici un plan de l'appartement de la famille Djamil:

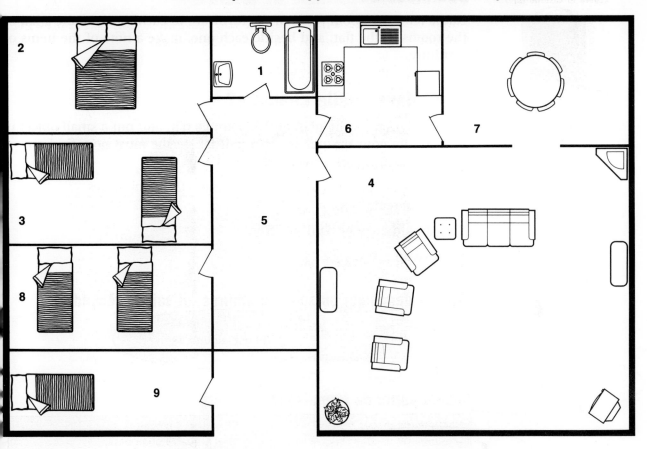

Ecoute la cassette (3)

Franck parle du plan de l'appartement

Franck names the rooms in the Djamils' flat. He gives each one a number.
Look at the plan above. Sketch it and label the rooms with their names.

Sais-tu parler des meubles?

Qu'y a-t-il dans la salle de bains?
    Il y a le W.C., le lavabo, et la baignoire.
Qu'y a-t-il dans la chambre de M. et Mme Djamil?
    Il y a un grand lit.
Qu'y a-t-il dans la chambre de Nadia et d'Annie?
    Il y a deux lits.
Qu'y a-t-il dans le salon?
    Il y a deux buffets, la télévision, un canapé, et trois fauteuils.
Qu'y a-t-il dans la chambre de Joseph et de Franck?
    Il y a deux lits.
Qu'y a-t-il dans le salon?
    Il y a une table et sept chaises.
Qu'y a-t-il dans la cuisine?
    Il y a un évier, la machine à laver et la cuisinière.

Ecoute la cassette (4)

Les meubles

Nadia tells you about some of the furniture in each room. Make a list of the rooms in the flat, and beside each one, make a note of the items of furniture.

C'est dans quelle chambre?

Et maintenant à toi

Choose a room in the plan of the Djamil's flat, and put a small object in it. Don't let your partner see where it is! He/she must now find out where it is, by asking questions:

> **e.g.** Il est dans la cuisine? Il est dans la chambre des parents? etc.

You should answer 'Oui' or 'Non'.

Then swap roles.

Sais-tu demander où sont les affaires, et sais-tu répondre?

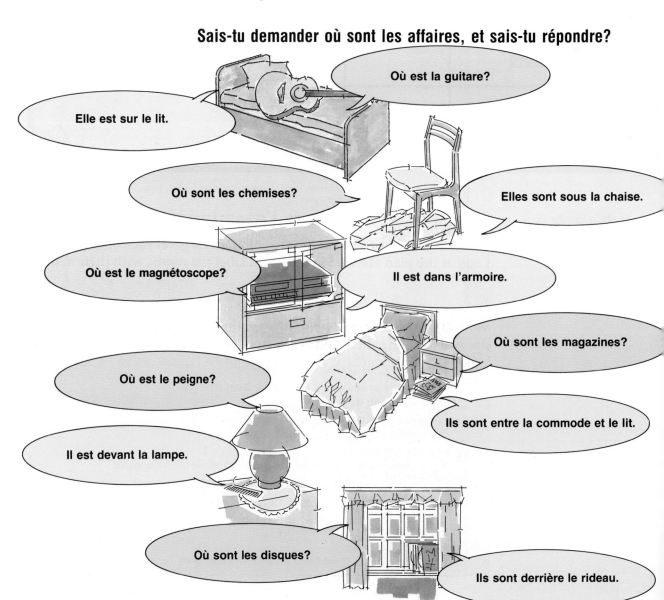

Et maintenant à toi

Où sont les affaires?

Practise the vocabulary by asking your partner where the various items are. Then draw similar pictures yourselves and ask each other questions about them.

Ecoute la cassette (5)

Les jeunes sont affreux!

Mme Djamil is talking about how untidy Nadia and Franck are. Here she is describing their bedrooms. Having listened to Mme Djamil, and looked at the pictures above, can you fill in the spaces in these sentences?

1   La guitare est . . . la commode.
   Les chaussettes sont sous le . . . .
   Les . . . sont sur l'ordinateur.
   Les livres sont . . . la robe de chambre.
   Le pyjama est . . . la chaise.

2   Le pantalon est . . . le lit et la commode.
   La veste est . . . l'ordinateur.
   Les chaussures sont . . . la table.
   La robe de chambre est . . . le placard.
   Le peigne est sur la . . . .

On trouve les différences

Your teacher will give you a drawing of a bedroom with objects in certain places. Your partner will have a picture of the same bedroom but the objects will be in different places.

Ask your partner where the following items are in his/her picture and say where they are in yours.

la guitare; les magazines; la veste; les disques; le pyjama; le pantalon; la cravate; les livres; les chaussettes; la robe de chambre.

A vous tous

On cache des objets

Trouvez l'objet caché

One person should go out of the room while the others hide an object. This person then returns, and should ask questions to find out where the object is hidden.

e.g. Il est sous la chaise?
Il est derrière le rideau?

When he/she has guessed correctly, he/she should hide the object for the next turn.

Sais-tu parler de ta chambre et des chambres de tes amis?

Dans ma chambre	il y a	mon lit. ma robe de chambre. mes livres.
Dans ta chambre	il y a	ton placard. ta guitare. tes vêtements.
Dans sa chambre	il y a	son pyjama. sa lampe. ses disques.

Ma chambre		petite. grande. agréable.
Sa chambre	est	déplaisante. sale. propre.
Ta chambre		en ordre. en désordre.

Ecoute la cassette (6)

Nadia et Franck décrivent leurs chambres

As Nadia and Franck talk about their rooms, try to make a list in your book of five words that describe each:

e.g.

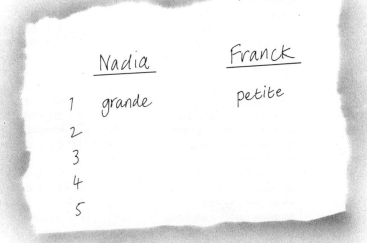

Nadia

Franck

1 grande   petite

2

3

4

5

Et maintenant à toi

Comment est ta chambre?

1   Ask your partner what his/her bedroom is like, and what is in it.
     Comment est ta chambre?
     Qu'y a-t-il dans ta chambre?
2   Make a note of his/her answers.
3   Talk to someone else, and tell them what your partner's room is like.

Sais-tu parler de tes animaux domestiques?

J'ai un chat. J'ai un chien. J'ai un poisson. J'ai un oiseau. J'ai une souris. J'ai un lapin. J'ai une tortue.	Mon chat est noir. Mon chien est grand.

Et maintenant à toi

On dessine des animaux

1   Draw one of the animals whose French name you know.
2   Your partner will ask you questions about what it is, its size and its colour. Following your answers, he/she will try to make a similar drawing.
3   Compare the two drawings, and then swap roles.
     The questions asked might go something like this:
     Comment est ton chat?
     Ton lapin est noir?
     Ta souris est petite?
     De quelle couleur est ton poisson?

Vocabulaire

affreux, affreuse	awful	**machine à laver** (f)	washing machine
agréable	nice, pleasant		
armoire (f)	cupboard	**magnétoscope** (m)	video recorder
baignoire (f)	bath	**meuble** (m)	item of furniture (usually in plural = furniture)
buffet (m)	sideboard		
cacher	to hide		
canapé (m)	settee, sofa	**oiseau** (m)	bird
chaise (f)	chair	**ordinateur** (m)	computer
chambre (f)	bedroom	**peigne** (m)	comb
chat (m)	cat	**pièce** (f)	room
chien (m)	dog	**poisson** (m)	fish
commode (f)	chest-of-drawers	**propre**	clean
cuisine (f)	kitchen	**pyjama** (m)	pyjamas
cuisinière (f)	cooker	**rideau** (m)	curtain
disque (m)	record	**robe de chambre** (f)	dressing-gown
déplaisant	nasty, unpleasant	**sale**	dirty
en désordre	untidy	**salle de bains** (f)	bathroom
en ordre	tidy	**salle de séjour** (f)	living-room
évier (m)	sink	**salle à manger** (f)	dining-room
fauteuil (m)	armchair	**salon** (m)	sitting-room
guitare (f)	guitar	**souris** (f)	mouse
lampe (f)	lamp	**table** (f)	table
lapin (m)	rabbit	**tortue** (f)	tortoise
lavabo (m)	washbasin	**télévision, télé** (f)	T.V.
lit (m)	bed	**vestibule** (m)	hall
livre (m)	book	**W.C.** (m)	toilet

UNITÉ 4

A boire et à manger

One of your jobs in the Djamil household is to give the children their meals. You therefore need to discover their likes and dislikes and go shopping for food.

At the end of this unit you should be able to:

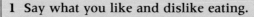

1 Say what you like and dislike eating.
2 Say at what time you eat different meals.
3 Offer and accept food at table.
4 Draw up a simple menu for children's meals.
5 Go shopping for everyday items of food.

Ecoute la cassette (1)

Ce qu'aiment Annie et Joseph

Annie and Joseph tell you what they like eating. Make a note so that you remember their favourite food.

	Annie	Joseph
1		
2		
3		
4		
5		

Sais-tu dire ce que tu aimes manger?

J'aime . . .	J'aime . . .	J'aime . . .
le bifteck	l'omelette	les bigmac
le jambon	la purée	les côtelettes
le poulet	la salade	de porc
le saucisson	la soupe	les saucisses
		les carottes
le gâteau		les frites
le pain (la	la glace	les haricots
baguette)	la tarte	verts
le fromage		les petits pois
le melon		les pommes de
le raisin		terre
		les œufs
le café	la bière	les sandwichs
le chocolat	la limonade	au pâté
le coca-cola		les tomates
le lait		
le thé		les biscuits
		les bonbons
		les bananes
		les pommes
		les oranges

Et maintenant à toi

Qu'est-ce que tu aimes manger?

1 Ask your partner what he/she likes to eat.
2 Ask two or three others.

Ecoute la cassette (2)

Et Nadia, qu'est-ce qu'elle aime?

Nadia tells you what she likes eating and what she doesn't like. Make a list of her likes and dislikes.

Nadia aime . . . Nadia n'aime pas . . .

Sais-tu dire ce que tu n'aimes pas manger?

J'aime le chocolat – je *n'*aime *pas* le chocolat.
Je mange le poulet – je *ne* mange *pas* le poulet.

Et maintenant à toi

Qu'est-ce que tu n'aimes pas manger?

1 Find out from your partner what he/she dislikes in the way of food.
2 Tell someone else about your partner's likes and dislikes.
3 Be ready to answer questions from your teacher or the French assistant.

Le Travail en Famille **37**

A vous tous

Un sondage

You are carrying out a mini-survey of your group's likes and dislikes.

1 Make a copy of the following table.

	Moi	1ère personne	2ème personne	3ème personne
les carottes les petits pois les pommes les bananes le thé le café la viande la salade le chou-fleur la soupe				

2 Ask and answer questions within the group:

   e.g. Tu aimes les carottes?

   If the answer is 'Oui', put a tick. If the answer is 'Non', put a cross.

3 Your teacher may then ask you:

   e.g. Qui aiment les carottes? or Combien de personnes aiment les carottes?

   You may then answer:

   e.g. Trois personnes aiment les carottes, etc.

   If no one likes carrots you will need to say:

   e.g. Personne n'aime les carottes.

4 When the whole class has answered, you can collect all the data and draw a bar chart showing how many like each thing.

Prends ton stylo

Ce que nous aimons

Using the information gained from the survey, write sentences in French about what you found.

Ecoute la cassette (3)

Ce que mangent les enfants Djamil

Although the children have already told you what they like and dislike, their mother is afraid that their diet may be rather strange if you only listen to them. She therefore tells you what they will and won't eat. Note down the details.

Et maintenant à toi

Ce que mange ta famille

Tell your partner what members of your own family will and won't eat. Your partner should note down the details.

Sais-tu parler des couverts?

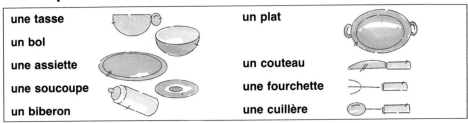

une tasse	un plat	
un bol		
une assiette	un couteau	
une soucoupe	une fourchette	
un biberon	une cuillère	

Ecoute la cassette (4)

Les heures des repas

Monsieur Djamil explains to you the times when the family usually eats. You decide to note this down and put the list up in your room. You plan to do this in French. Copy out the sentences and fill in the gaps.

La famille Djamil prend le petit déjeuner à .... heures.
Ils prennent le déjeuner normalement à .... heure.
Les enfants prennent le goûter à .... heures.
Tout le monde sauf Joseph prend le dîner à .... heures.

Ecoute la cassette (5)

Déjeuner chez les Djamil

It is lunchtime in the Djamil household. You are offered some food. Can you note down exactly what you are offered? There are five items.

Sais-tu proposer à manger et accepter ou refuser?

Tu prends du gâteau?
Vous prenez du gâteau?

Ah oui, je veux bien.

Tu veux du chocolat?
Vous voulez du chocolat?

Ah oui, je veux bien.

Vous prenez de la soupe?

Ah oui, je veux bien.

Vous voulez de la glace?

Non, merci.

Tu prends des pommes de terre?

Non, merci.

Tu veux encore de chou-fleur?

Non, merci, ça suffit.

Et maintenant à toi

On te propose à manger

1 Work with your partner. Offer him/her some food and reply to what he/she offers. (You could use pictures for this if you like).
2 If possible, offer your teacher or the assistant something. Remember to say '**vous**' when talking to adults other than family or friends.

Un peu de lecture

Le menu de Nadia

Nadia has written out the lunch menu. Will you like what you are going to eat?

Déjeuner
soupe à l'oignon
côtelettes de porc avec
purée de pommes de terre
fromage
fruits

Prends ton stylo

Ton menu à toi

Next time it's your turn to write out the menu. Using the list of food items on page 36, choose what you will have and write the menu out in French.

Ecoute la cassette (6)

Les commissions de M. Djamil

Monsieur Djamil sends you and Franck shopping. Copy out the incomplete sentences. Then listen and complete them.

1 A la boulangerie on achète ....   **2** A la boucherie on achète ....

3 A l'épicerie on achète ....   **4** A la pharmacie on achète ....

Sais-tu demander ce qu'il te faut? . . . et comprendre la réponse?

Les envies de Joseph

Un peu de lecture

One day when you take Joseph shopping with you he wants several items that he sees.

Answer these questions about the cheese and the felt pens he fancies.

1 How much is the cheese?
2 How many pieces do you get?
3 What is there in the cheese that might be good for Joseph?
4 What extra item is there in the box
   to encourage children to want it?

5 Is the ink in the felt pens permanent or will it wash out of his clothes if he makes a mess?

6 What extra-special pen is there?

Et maintenant à toi

Tu fais les achats

1 Take turns to pick a card and to ask your partner for the item. You will say 'Je voudrais . . . ., s'il vous plaît' as if your partner were a shopkeeper.

2 Now do the same thing with several cards. After each request the shopkeeper should say 'Et encore?' When you have finished your list you will say 'C'est tout, merci'.

Ecoute la cassette (7)

Ça fait cinq francs

At the grocer's you are behind a young woman in the queue. Out of interest you note the prices of the things she wants to buy.

Sais-tu demander et donner les prix?

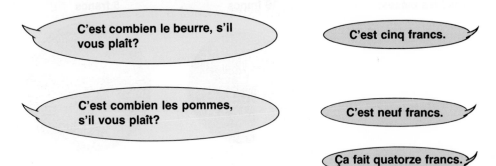

Un peu de lecture

Au supermarché

You have just done some shopping at the supermarket and, before you take the wrappings off the fruit and veg. you bought, you make a note, in English, of each item and what it cost so that you can account for it later.

FRUITS & LEGUMES		
POMME DE TERRE		
kg	F/kg	F
0,620	3,25	2,00

FRUITS & LEGUMES		
CHAMPIGNON		
kg	F/kg	F
0,130	19,50	2,55

FRUITS & LEGUMES		
PECHE JAUNE		
kg	F/kg	F
0,280	8,90	2,50

FRUITS & LEGUMES		
RAISIN		
kg	F/kg	F
0,305	11,50	3,50

Et maintenant à toi

C'est combien?

Travaille avec un collègue.

Take turns to turn over a card and ask the price. Your partner turns over a card from a second pile and tells you the price.

C'est combien l'eau minérale, s'il vous plaît?

C'est cinq francs.

Sais-tu comment utiliser l'argent français?

Voici les pièces:

10 francs   5 francs

2 francs   1 franc

½ (50 centimes)   20 centimes

10 centimes)   5 centimes

N.B. 1 franc = 100 centimes

1 franc vaut approximativement 10p, donc 10 francs vaut à peu près £1. (Evidemment ceci peut varier selon le marché.)

Voici les billets quotidiens:

200 francs   100 francs

50 francs   20 francs

Sais-tu compter jusqu'à 100?

70	soixante-dix	80	quatre vingts
71	soixante-onze	81	quatre-vingt-un
72	soixante-douze	82	quatre-vingt-deux
73	soixante-treize	83	quatre-vingt-trois
74	soixante-quatorze	84	quatre-vingt-quatre
75	soixante-quinze	85	quatre-vingt-cinq
76	soixante-seize	86	quatre-vingt-six
77	soixante-dix-sept	87	quatre-vingt-sept
78	soixante-dix-huit	88	quatre-vingt-huit
79	soixante-dix-neuf	89	quatre-vingt-neuf
90	quatre-vingt-dix	95	quatre-vingt-quinze
91	quatre-vingt-onze	96	quatre-vingt-seize
92	quatre-vingt-douze	97	quatre-vingt-dix-sept
93	quatre-vingt-treize	98	quatre-vingt-dix-huit
94	quatre-vingt-quatorze	99	quatre-vingt-dix-neuf
		100	cent

Un peu de lecture

Au centre distributeur

You go to do some personal shopping at a large hypermarket. Madame Djamil has asked you to get a few food items as well. She wants cheese, bread, coffee and eggs. List the items and prices to work out what she owes you.

Ecoute la cassette (8)

Et maintenant à toi

A l'épicerie

Listen carefully to this conversation.

A l'épicerie encore

1 Try to repeat the conversation with your partner.
2 Try the following:

Le client/la cliente	Le marchand/la marchande
Say hello. Ask for one kilo of apples. Say that's all and ask how much it is. Pay and say goodbye.	Say hello. Say of course and ask if there is anything else. Say it's four francs. Say thanks and goodbye.

3 Now try and make up some more conversations. You could use the grocery cards again if you like.

Vocabulaire

aimer	to like	**melon** (*m*)	melon
arriver	to arrive	**œuf** (*m*)	egg
assiette (*f*)	plate	**oignon** (*m*)	onion
baguette (*f*)	French stick (bread)	**omelette** (*f*)	omelette
banane (*f*)	banana	**orange** (*f*)	orange
beurre (*m*)	butter	**pain** (*m*)	bread
biberon (*m*)	baby's bottle	**paquet** (*m*)	packet
bifteck (*m*)	steak	**petits pois** (*m*)	peas
bigmac (*m*)	McDonald's hamburger	**pharmacie** (*f*)	chemist's shop
biscuit (*m*)	biscuit	**plat** (*m*)	serving dish
bière (*f*)	beer	**pomme** (*f*)	apple
bol (*m*)	bowl	**pomme de terre** (*f*)	potato
bonbon (*m*)	sweet	**porc** (*m*)	pork
boucherie (*f*)	butcher's shop	**poulet** (*m*)	chicken
boulangerie (*f*)	baker's shop	**prendre**	to take, have (a meal)
boîte (*f*)	box, tin	**purée** (*f*)	mashed potato
café (*m*)	coffee	**pâté** (*m*)	meat paste
carotte (*f*)	carrot	**pêche** (*f*)	peach
cerise (*f*)	cherry	**raisin** (*m*)	grape(s)
champignon (*m*)	mushroom	**regarder**	to look at, watch
chocolat (*m*)	chocolate	**regretter**	to be sorry
chou-fleur (*f*)	cauliflower	**rentrer**	to return home
coca-cola (*m*)	coca-cola	**salade** (*f*)	salad
couteau (*m*)	knife	**sandwich** (*m*)	sandwich
cuillère (*f*)	spoon	**saucisse** (*f*)	sausage
côtelette (*f*)	cutlet, chop (meat)	**saucisson** (*m*)	salami
demi-kilo (*m*)	half-kilo	**se coucher**	to go to bed
faire	to do, to make	**se lever**	to get up
fourchette (*f*)	fork	**se réveiller**	to wake up
frite (*f*)	chip	**soucoupe** (*f*)	saucer
fromage (*m*)	cheese	**soupe** (*f*)	soup
glace (*f*)	ice-cream	**tarte** (*f*)	tart
gâteau (*m*)	cake	**tasse** (*f*)	cup
haricots verts (*m*)	beans	**thé** (*m*)	tea
jambon (*m*)	ham	**tomate** (*f*)	tomato
lait (*m*)	milk	**viande** (*f*)	meat
limonade (*f*)	lemonade	**vin** (*m*)	wine
manger	to eat		

UNITÉ 5

La journée en famille

You learn about the daily routine of members of the Djamil family and also about your own household duties, particularly those to do with looking after the younger children.

At the end of this unit you should be able to:

1 Talk about your daily routine.
2 Tell the time in hours and half hours.
3 Talk about minor health problems.
4 Give simple instructions to children.
5 Understand some childish terms for everyday things.

Ecoute la cassette (1)

La journée de Franck

Listen while Franck tells you what he does during the day. Make a note of the time and the activity he describes:

Il se lève . . .
Il prend le petit déjeuner . . .
Il quitte la maison . . .
Il arrive à l'école . . .
Il prend le déjeuner . . .

Il rentre à la maison . . .
Il joue au football . . .
Il prend le dîner . . .
Il va au club . . .
Il se couche . . .

Sais-tu dire ce que tu fais le matin?

A sept heures
je me réveille

A sept heures et quart
je me lève
et je m'habille

A sept heures et demie
je fais ma toilette . . .
je me lave
je me coiffe
je me brosse les dents
. . . et les cheveux

A huit heures moins le quart
je prends le petit déjeuner

. . . et à quelle heure tu fais certaines choses?

J'arrive à l'école	à neuf heures
Je prends le déjeuner	à midi
Je rentre à la maison	à quatre heures
Je regarde la télé	à cinq heures
Je prends le dîner	à six heures
Je fais mes devoirs	à sept heures
Je me couche	à dix heures

Et maintenant à toi

Qu'est-ce que tu fais à . . .?

Work with your partner. Your teacher will give each of you a set of cards, one set contains times and the other activities.
One of you turns over a time card and says:
   e.g. Qu'est-ce que tu fais à sept heures?
The other turns over an activity card and says:
   e.g. Je me lève.
Take turns to ask and answer questions

Ecoute la cassette (2)

La matinée d'Annie

Listen as Annie tells you what she does each morning, and put the following sentences in the right order by numbering them.

   A sept heures elle va à la cuisine.
   Elle quitte l'appartement à sept heures et demie.
   Annie se réveille à six heures.
   Elle fait sa toilette dans la salle de bains.
   Elle prend son petit déjeuner.
   Elle se lève à six heures et demie.
   Elle s'habille dans sa chambre.
   Elle se brosse les cheveux.

Prends ton stylo

Décris ta journée

   e.g. Je me réveille à six heures.

Sais-tu parler du travail de ta journée?

Je fais le ménage:

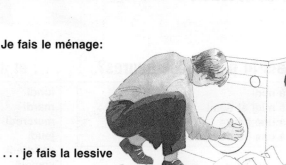

. . . je fais la lessive

. . . je fais la vaisselle

. . . je passe l'aspirateur   . . . je fais les lits    . . . je repasse le linge

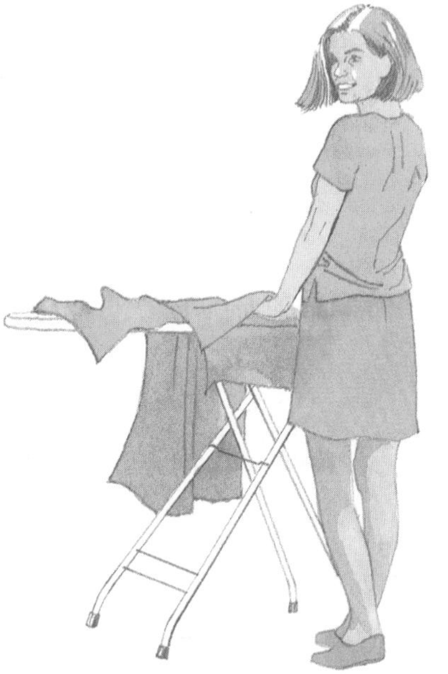

Je mets la table

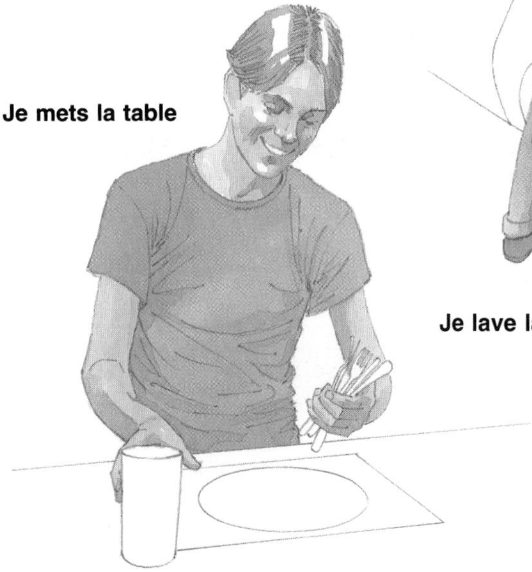

Je prépare
le goûter

Je lave la voiture

Je fais les courses

Sais-tu parler des heures?   . . . et des jours de la semaine?

à midi	lundi
à midi et demi	mardi
à une heure	mercredi
à une heure et demie	jeudi
	vendredi
	samedi
	dimanche

Et maintenant à toi

A dix heures . . .

1 Ask your partner what he/she does during the day, and make a note of the answer for your partner to check.

> **e.g.** Qu'est-ce que tu fais à dix heures le samedi?

2 Answer your partner's questions about your day.

> **e.g.** Je lave la voiture.

Prends ton stylo

Le samedi

Franck is interested in what you do on Saturdays at home. Make a list in French to show him.

> **e.g.** A onze heures je fais les courses.

Et maintenant à toi

Vivre son weekend

Take the list your partner made in the exercise above, and explain to someone else what he/she does on a Saturday.

> **e.g.** A onze heures il/elle fait les courses.

Sais-tu donner des ordres?

Dépêche-toi	**Dépêchez-vous**
Lève-toi	**Levez-vous**
Lave-toi	**Lavez-vous**
Aide-moi	**Aidez-moi**
Réveille-toi	**Réveillez-vous**
Mets la table	**Mettez la table**
Habille-toi	**Habillez-vous**
Tais-toi	**Taisez-vous**
Fais la vaisselle	**Faites la vaisselle**
Lave la voiture	**Lavez la voiture**
Ecoute	**Ecoutez**
Prépare le biberon	**Préparez le biberon**
Range tes jouets	**Rangez vos jouets**
Cherche la sucette	**Cherchez la sucette**

Ecoute la cassette (3)

Monsieur Djamil donne des ordres

Listen to the cassette and write down who is being told to do what. You might find it useful to draw a grid like the one below.

	Franck	Nadia	Annie	Joseph
do hair				
wake up				
get up				
have a wash				
lay the table				
get dressed				
be quiet				
hurry up				
eat your bread				
put away your bowls				
wash up				
make your bed				
help Joseph				

Travaillez en groupe

Donner des ordres

Take turns to give orders and mime the actions.

e.g. Susie, lave la voiture!

Susie mimes washing a car, and then says:

e.g. John, prépare le café!

Un peu de lecture

Quel département?

One Saturday M. Djamil takes you, Franck and Nadia for a drive in the country in the family car.

You are curious to know what the numbers on the registration plates on French cars mean. Franck explains that the last two figures indicate the area (**département**) where the car was registered. So, the 31 on their car indicates the Haute Garonne, the **département** where Toulouse is situated. These figures are also used as part of the postcode on letters. He also explains that France is divided into **départements** just as England is divided into counties, and shows you a map which marks them and their numbers.

1 How many **départements** can you pick out that are named after geographical features (mountains, seas, rivers)?

2 Look at the six number-plates and see if you can spot where each vehicle comes from.

Ecoute la cassette (4)

Le cabinet du Docteur Djamil

Mme Djamil is a doctor. Occasionally you help her by answering the telephone. Some of her patients ring up. Make a note in your book of what is wrong with each one.

Mme Azouté _____ M. Leblanc _____

Mme Bonnet _____ M. Bensaïd _____

Sais-tu dire que ça ne va pas?

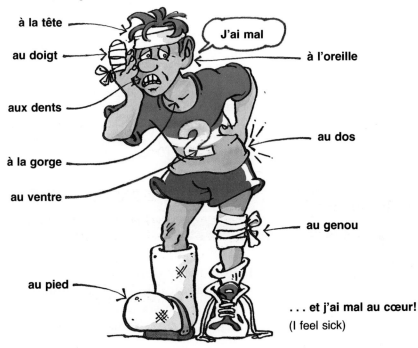

Sais-tu parler des maladies d'enfant?

la rougeole	measles
la rubéole	German measles
la varicelle	chicken pox
la coqueluche	whooping cough
les oreillons	mumps

Travaillez en groupe

Devinez la maladie

Each person writes the name of an ailment on a piece of paper, without showing it to the others. The other members of the group take turns to guess what is wrong.

e.g. Tu as mal à la gorge? – Non.
Tu as mal au dos?

The person who guesses correctly takes the next turn as the patient.

Sais-tu comprendre les enfants?

faire pipi	tonton	bobo	bisou
aller au dodo	tata	peton	nounours
mamy	minou	joujoux	la frimousse
papy	toutou	câlin	les pattes

Ecoute la cassette (5)

Les phrases enfantines

Listen to these people who are using childish expressions. Link the numbers on the tape with the pictures below.

a

b

c

d

e

f

g

h

i

j

Un peu de lecture

L'agenda du jour

M. and Mme Djamil and Nadia have gone out for the day leaving you with Annie and Joseph. Mme Djamil has left you a list of things she wants done. Rewrite the list in the order in which you intend to do the jobs.

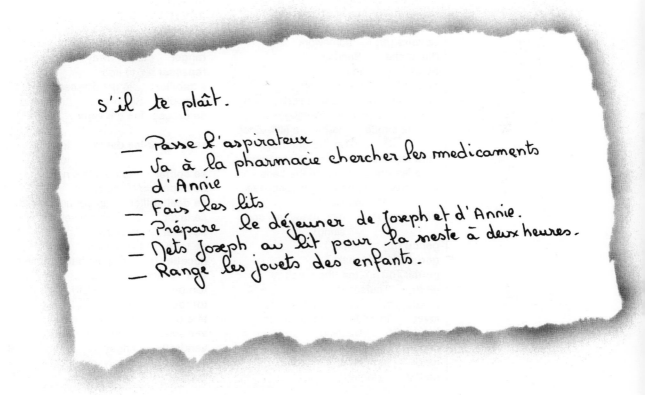

S'il te plaît.

— Passe l'aspirateur
— Va à la pharmacie chercher les medicaments d'Annie
— Fais les lits
— Prépare le déjeuner de Joseph et d'Annie.
— Mets Joseph au lit pour la sieste à deux heures.
— Range les jouets des enfants.

Prends ton stylo

Une lettre à un ami

You decide to write to your pen-friend in Paris telling him about your life with the Djamil family. In it you list what Joseph does each day and what you have to do. Write that part of the letter in French. Write 6 to 8 sentences. You could start with:

Joseph se réveille à six heures, il . . .

Ecoute la cassette (6)

Les problèmes de Joëlle

A French girl whom you have met phones you one day. She looks after two little girls called Béatrice and Agathe, and she seems to be having a few problems. When you write home you decide to re-tell this sad story. Make a few notes in English to help you.

Vocabulaire

aller au dodo	to go to bed/sleep (baby talk)
aspirateur (*m*)	vacuum-cleaner
avoir bobo	to have a pain, be hurt (baby talk)
avoir mal	to have a pain, be hurt
bisou (*m*)	kiss (baby talk)
bobo (*m*)	hurt/pain (baby talk)
cœur (*m*)	heart;
j'ai mal au cœur	I feel sick
câlin (*m*)	cuddle (baby talk)
dent (*f*)	tooth
devoirs (*m*)	homework
dimanche	Sunday
doigt (*m*)	finger
dos (*m*)	back
déjeuner (*m*)	lunch, midday meal
dîner (*m*)	dinner, evening meal
faire la sieste	to have a little sleep in the afternoon
faire les courses	to go shopping
faire les lits	to make the beds
faire pipi	to do a 'wee' (baby talk and slang)
frimousse (*f*)	face (baby talk and slang)
genou (*m*)	knee
gorge (*f*)	throat
goûter (*m*)	tea (the meal)
jeudi	Thursday
joujou (*m*)	toy (baby talk)
laver	to wash (something)
lessive (*f*)	washing
linge (*m*)	clothes, underwear
lundi	Monday
mamy	granny
mardi	Tuesday
mercredi	Wednesday
mettre la table	to lay the table
minou	pussy cat
nounours (*m*)	teddy bear
oreille (*f*)	ear
papy	grandpa
patte (*f*)	animal's paw/hand in baby talk
peton (*m*)	foot (baby talk)
pied (*m*)	foot
préparer	to prepare
quitter	to leave
ranger	to put away
repasser	to iron
s'habiller	to get dressed
samedi	Saturday
se brosser les cheveux	to brush one's hair
se brosser les dents	to brush one's teeth
se coiffer	to do one's hair
se dépêcher	to hurry
se déshabiller	to get undressed
se laver	to wash oneself
se raser	to shave
se taire	to be quiet
sucette (*f*)	lollipop, baby's dummy
tata	auntie (familiar)
tonton	uncle (familiar)
toutou	doggy
tête (*f*)	head
vaisselle (*f*)	crockery, washing up
vendredi	Friday
ventre (*m*)	belly, stomach
voiture (*f*)	car

2 DEUXIÈME PARTIE

L'Hôtellerie

This section is about working in a hotel. You are on a work experience placement, learning how to do some of the tasks in the kitchens, the restaurant and the reception area, as well as some of the domestic duties in the bedrooms and utility rooms.

Your placement is in the Hôtel de la Poste, a 2-star hotel in Châteauroux where M. and Mme Cheritweitzer are the proprietors.

UNITÉ 1

On achète des provisions

. *When you first start work at the Hôtel de la Poste, you are sent out to the local shops to buy food for the restaurant.*

At the end of this unit you should be able to:

1 Understand spoken and written instructions concerning the purchase of food and drink.
2 Use expressions of quantity.
3 Understand and use French currency.
4 Ask for foodstuffs in shops, markets, and supermarkets.

Ecoute la cassette (1)

Les marchands du quartier

Some local shopkeepers are in the bar of the Hôtel de la Poste. They introduce themselves to you. Can you work out where each one works?

Tu as trouvé les bonnes réponses?

Sais-tu parler des marchands et des magasins?

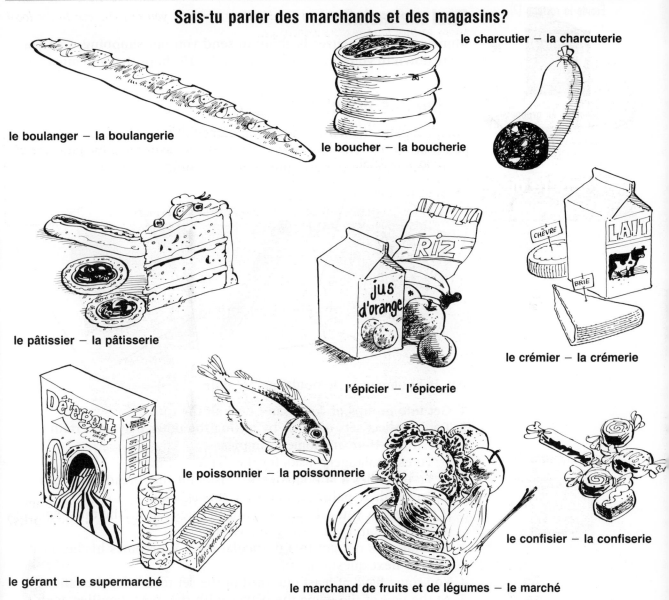

le charcutier – la charcuterie

le boulanger – la boulangerie

le boucher – la boucherie

le pâtissier – la pâtisserie

l'épicier – l'épicerie

le crémier – la crémerie

le poissonnier – la poissonnerie

le confisier – la confiserie

le gérant – le supermarché

le marchand de fruits et de légumes – le marché

Et maintenant à toi

Où faut-il aller?

Work with a partner, using the cards that your teacher gives you. Place the cards in a pile face downwards. Take one card from the top, and tell your partner that you want the item shown. Your partner should then tell you which shop to go to.

e.g.

Je voudrais du chocolat.

Va à la confiserie!

Take turns to do this, until you have worked through the cards.

Ecoute la cassette (2)

Travaillez en groupe

Quel magasin?

Monsieur Cheritweitzer is about to send you out shopping. Can you write down in your book the names of the 10 shops that you must go to?

Le jeu des marchands

This is a game which practises the names of food shops, shopkeepers and food items. The aim is to collect sets of cards each containing one shop, one shopkeeper and one item you could buy there:

e.g. la boulangerie, le boulanger, le pain.

1 Get into groups of 4 or 5 and deal all the cards.
2 Try to collect sets of cards by asking the other players certain questions. Here are some examples:
    'Tu es boulanger?' asks for the 'baker' card.
    'Tu travailles à la boulangerie?' asks for the 'bread shop' card.
    'Tu vends le pain?' asks for the 'bread' card.
   If the person you ask has the card in question he/she must hand it over to you and you can go on asking.
3 If he/she has not got that particular card, it becomes his/her turn to ask the next question.
4 You must have at least one card of the set to ask for the others.
5 At the end of the game the player with the most 'families' is the winner.

Sais-tu ce qu'ils vendent en plus?

Le boulanger vend le pain,
          la baguette,
          le croissant.
	Le boucher vend le porc,
	          les biftecks,
	          l'agneau.

Le charcutier vend le saucisson,
          le jambon,
          les plats cuisinés.
	Le crémier vend le lait,
	          le beurre,
	          le fromage,
	          les œufs,
	          le yaourt.

Le poissonnier vend le poisson.
          la truite,
          la morue.
	Le pâtissier vend les gâteaux,
	          les tartes.

Ecoute la cassette (3)

On fait les courses

Mme Cheritweitzer sends you shopping. She wants several things from different shops.

You have already prepared a 'self-help' shopping pad which could look like this:

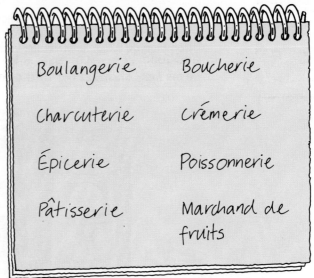

Boulangerie   Boucherie

Charcuterie   Crémerie

Épicerie   Poissonnerie

Pâtisserie   Marchand de fruits

Make a note of the things that Mme Cheritweitzer wants, under the shops where you will buy them.

Sais-tu demander où tu peux acheter des choses?

. . . et sais-tu répondre?

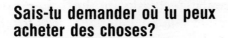

Où est-ce que je peux acheter du pain?

. . . à la boulangerie.

Où est-ce que je peux acheter des bonbons?

. . . à la confiserie.

Prends ton stylo

La liste d'achats

Make a shopping list of 10 items in French.

Et maintenant à toi

Où est-ce qu'on peut acheter?

Ask your partner where you can buy the items from the shopping list you have just made.

Write down the answers in English and check with someone else (or the teacher) that these answers are correct:

e.g. On achète du lait à la crémerie, n'est-ce pas? − Oui, c'est vrai.

Sais-tu demander les quantités de solides, et de liquides?

Les liquides s'achètent par **litres** (ou **demi-litres**).

Les solides s'achètent par **grammes** et **kilogrammes (kilos).**
(Un paquet de sucre pèse un kilo).

Beaucoup de choses s'achètent selon leur empaquetage:

Combien de .... **voulez-vous?**
.... **veux-tu?**
Il me faut ....

un paquet

une boîte

une bouteille

Ecoute la cassette (4)

Et maintenant à toi

Travaillez en groupe

Combien il en faut?

Mme Cheritweitzer has just remembered that she hasn't told you how much she wants of each of the things that you have marked on your pad. Write them down as she tells you.

Combien en voulez-vous?

Make another shopping list and, on a separate sheet, mark how much of each item you want.

Give the shopping list to your partner, who will play the part of the shopkeeper and ask you how much you want of each item. When he/she has written this information down, check that it is correct. Then change roles.

Le jeu de Loto

You play this game like Bingo. One person should be the caller.
1 The others in the group should each choose a different **Loto** card.
2 The caller will announce the items shown on the cards, using the set of smaller cards which the teacher will provide.
3 Block off the items on your card when they are called. The first player to completely block off his/her card is the winner.

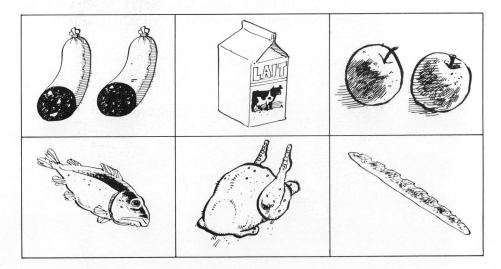

Sais-tu compter jusqu'à 1000?

200 = deux cents	**201 = deux cent un** **202 = deux cent deux** . . . . etc
300 = trois cents	**320 = trois cent vingt** **367 = trois cent soixante-sept** . . . . etc
. . . . etc **1000 = mille**	

Ecoute la cassette (5)

A la boucherie

M. Cheritweitzer has sent you to check on the price of meat in the two local butchers' shops. First, listen to M. Auroch, one of the butchers. Can you recognise the prices as he tells them to you?

The other butcher, M. Boyer, has not yet marked his prices in his shop window. Note them down when he tells you what they are.

Now make a list in order to tell M. Cheritweitzer where each meat is cheaper. Write the name of the butcher whose meat is cheaper beside each item.

Et maintenant à toi

C'est quoi ça?

Look at the market stalls and shop displays shown here. Check that you know the names of the items for sale:

e.g. Indique les bonbons!   Voici les bonbons.
Indique une boîte d'oranges!   Voici une boîte d'oranges.

Ecoute la cassette (7)

Les prix

Each trader is announcing his prices. Mark them on the card that your teacher gives you, and keep the card safely. You will need it again.

la pâtisserie		

Sais-tu demander poliment ce qu'il te faut?

Client	Marchand
Bonjour, Monsieur .... Je voudrais .... Je voudrais aussi	Bonjour, etc. Bien sûr! Voila! Et avec ça? Voilà! C'est tout?
Oui, c'est tout. Combien je vous dois?	Alors, les .... 20 francs, les .... 10f.50, etc. En tout ça
Voilà! Merci! Au revoir!	fait ....

Ecoute la cassette (8)

Au marché

You have been sent to the local market to check on the day's prices. M. Cheritweitzer often buys fruit and vegetables here, and wants to know the price today of:

pommes   petits pois
oranges   pommes de terre
pêches   haricots verts
bananes   salade verte

Note down the prices of other items that you hear the stallholders announce.

Travaillez en groupe

Vous désirez?

Use the card on which you marked the prices.

Choose a partner who has a different card from yours. Go into his/her 'shop' and buy some foodstuffs. Then wait for him/her to buy some things from your shop.

Now find another partner who has a different shop, and buy some things from him/her. Continue with other partners, until you have been to all six shops.

Vocabulaire

agneau (m)	lamb	**gâteau** (m)	cake
bonbons (m)	sweets	**magasin** (m)	shop
boucher (m)	butcher	**marchand** (m)	shopkeeper
boucherie (f)	butcher's shop	**marché** (m)	market
boulanger (m)	baker	**merguez** (m)	highly-spiced sausage
boulangerie (f)	baker's shop	**morue** (f)	cod
charcuterie (f)	delicatessen, cooked-meat shop	**plat cuisiné** (m)	ready-cooked dish
charcutier (m)	pork-butcher	**poisson** (m)	fish
confiserie (f)	sweetshop	**poissonnerie** (f)	fish shop (wet fish)
confisier (f)	confectioner (sweets)	**poissonnier** (m)	fishmonger
croissant (m)	crescent-shaped roll	**pâtisserie** (f)	cake shop
crémier (m)	dairy shopkeeper	**pâtissier** (m)	confectioner (cakes)
crémerie (f)	dairy shop	**saucisson** (m)	salami
épicerie (f)	grocer's shop	**supermarché** (m)	supermarket
épicier (m)	grocer	**tarte** (f)	tart
gérant (m)	manager	**truite** (f)	trout
		yaourt (m)	yoghurt

UNITÉ 2

On travaille à la cuisine

During your time at the Hôtel de la Poste, you are given the chance to gain experience in the kitchen as a trainee chef.

At the end of this unit you should be able to:

1 Understand and use certain simple terms for cooking.
2 Deal with quantities in weights and measures.
3 Use the words for the most important utensils.
4 Understand some terms used on French menus.

Ecoute la cassette (1)

Aider le chef

The chef is telling you how you can be of help to him. These picture show the jobs you must do. Write down the letters in the order in which you hear the jobs mentioned.

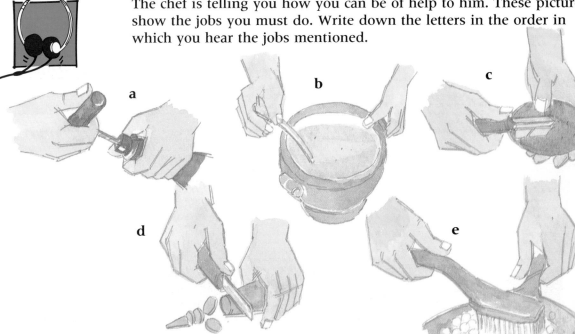

Sais-tu ce qu'il te faut pour faire la cuisine?

le sel	l'ail l'huile	le beurre
le poivre	les fines herbes	le vinaigre	la moutarde

Et maintenant à toi

Les ingrédients

Work with your partner. You will be given five **cartes d'ingrédients**. Place them face down between you. Take turns to turn over a card. Your partner asks, in French, for the item shown on the card. If he/she asks correctly, give him/her the card. The person with most cards at the end is the winner.

e.g. Le sel, s'il te plaît?
Voici le sel.

La moutarde, s'il te plaît?
Non, je regrette.

Sais-tu ce qui se trouve dans la cuisine?

l'étagère

le frigo

la cuisinière

le placard

l'armoire

l'évier

le tiroir

le congélateur   le four   la table   la poubelle

. . . et les noms des ustensiles de cuisine?

une casserole	saucepan
une soupière	soup tureen
un grand couteau	large knife
une planche à hâcher	chopping-board
un tire-bouchon	corkscrew
un ouvre-boîtes	tin-opener
une râpe à fromage	cheese-grater
une poêle	frying pan
une louche	ladle
un tablier	apron
une cuiller, cuillère	spoon
un mixer	mixer
un robot de cuisine	food processor

Ecoute la cassette (2)

Où se trouve . . . ?

The chef asks you to pass him some utensils. Write down where to find everything.

Et maintenant à toi

Trouver les objets

Work with your partner. One of you has been given a picture showing where everything is in the kitchen. The other has the same picture but with certain items listed underneath instead of in the picture. He/she should ask where these items are:

e.g. Où est le sel?
Il est sur l'étagère, à gauche de la cuisinière.

Sais-tu utiliser les expressions culinaires?

mélanger	to mix	**éplucher**	to peel
ajouter	to add	**râper**	to grate
une demi-cuillerée	dessert-spoonful	**tourner**	to turn, mix
une petite cuillerée	tea-spoonful	**remuer**	to stir
une grande cuillerée	table-spoonful	**mijoter**	to simmer
une pincée de	pinch of	**faire cuire**	to cook
cinq cent grammes de	500 grams of	**griller**	to grill
un litre de	litre of	**faire frire**	to fry
un coquetier	egg-cup	**faire bouillir**	to boil
l'eau bouillante	boiling water	**verser**	to pour
des morceaux	pieces	**couper**	to cut, slice
faire fondre	to melt or dissolve	**assaisonner**	to season

Un peu de lecture

Une recette

Read this recipe. Can you work out what is being prepared?

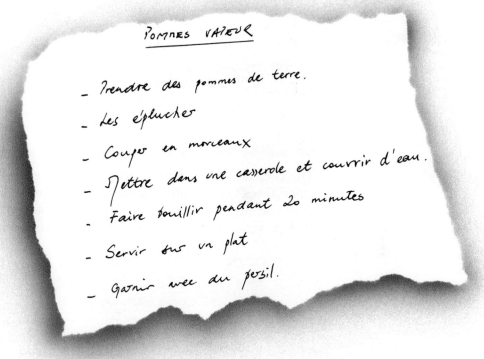

POMMES VAPEUR

- Prendre des pommes de terre.
- Les éplucher
- Couper en morceaux
- Mettre dans une casserole et couvrir d'eau.
- Faire bouillir pendant 20 minutes
- Servir sur un plat
- Garnir avec du persil.

Ecoute la cassette (3)

La vinaigrette

The chef has decided to trust you to prepare a salad-dressing, (**une vinaigrette**). Listen and make notes as he gives you your instructions.

Prends ton stylo

Une recette vite faite

Write out a simple recipe in French. You could describe how to boil an egg, or make a cup of coffee.

If you have time, do another recipe for something simple.

Travaillez en groupe

Jeu de recettes

Each person in the group will receive a **carte de recette** and several **cartes d'ingrédients** which represent the items needed to prepare the meal. Each person asks in turn for an item he/she requires for that meal.

e.g. Tu as le sel, Diane?

If the person asked has the '**sel**' card it must be handed over and the questioner has another turn. If not, the turn passes to the next person. The first person to have all the required ingredients is the winner.

Ecoute la cassette (4)

Préparer un croque-monsieur

During a quiet moment in the kitchen where you are working you fancy a snack! You ask one of the cooks how to make a **croque-monsieur**. Listen as he tells you and note down what he says.

Un peu de lecture

La sauce ravigote

The chef has asked you to prepare a **sauce ravigote** for one of his 'specialités'! Fortunately he has written down all the instructions. Make sure you understand them – you don't want to go wrong now he has trusted you – it could be back to the washing up!

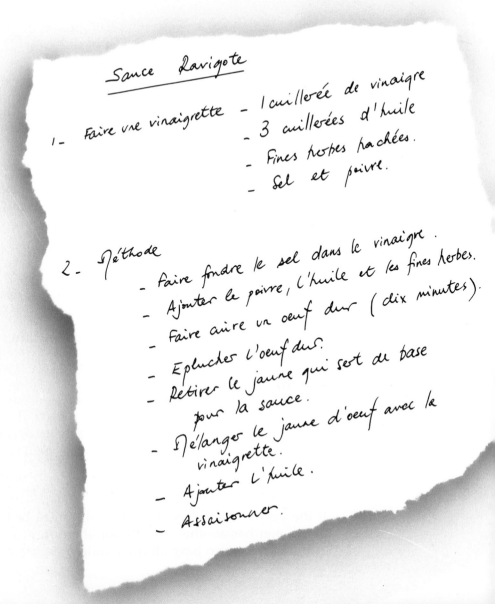

Sauce Ravigote

1 - Faire une vinaigrette
 - 1 cuillerée de vinaigre
 - 3 cuillerées d'huile
 - Fines herbes hachées.
 - Sel et poivre.

2 - Méthode
 - Faire fondre le sel dans le vinaigre.
 - Ajouter le poivre, l'huile et les fines herbes.
 - Faire cuire un oeuf dur (dix minutes).
 - Eplucher l'oeuf dur.
 - Retirer le jaune qui sert de base pour la sauce.
 - Mélanger le jaune d'oeuf avec la vinaigrette.
 - Ajouter l'huile.
 - Assaisonner.

Sais-tu comment s'appellent les viandes?

l'agneau	le steak
le bifteck	l'entrecôte
le bœuf	le mouton
le canard	le lapin
le poulet	le porc
les escargots	les cuisses de grenouilles

Préfères-tu le poisson ou les coquillages?

la morue	la crabe
le maquereau	les moules
les fruits de mer	la truite
les sardines	le sole
les huîtres	la raie

Ecoute la cassette (5)

Enfin, qu'est-ce qu'ils aiment?

A group of young people are staying for the week in the Hôtel de la Poste. As they have done nothing but complain about the food prepared by the chef, he asks you to find out what they do like. He would ask them himself but, like all great artists, he is sulking a little. Try to help. Note down each person's favourite food.

Et maintenant à toi

Ils aiment ça

Work with your partner. Imagine that he/she is the chef and report back what the young people have just told you.

e.g. Dans le groupe trois personnes aiment la soupe, etc.

Your partner will note down the details – tonight they will eat!

Prends ton stylo

Le menu des jeunes

In view of what the young people have told you, it should not be too difficult to give them something they could all eat. Write out tonight's special **menu des jeunes** in French. Take some time to present it well. Use a word processor if one is available.

Travaillez en groupe

Le sondage gastronomique

Find out what each person in your group likes to eat. When everyone has answered put the results down in the form of a table, and be ready to report the findings of your survey to the other groups.

e.g. Qu'est-ce que tu aimes?

Mary	poulet – frites – glace
John	frites – boeuf – hamburgers
Carl	poulet – boeuf – glace
Elaine	poulet – poisson – frites

For the report-back you could say:

> **e.g.** Dans notre groupe trois personnes aiment le poulet;
> trois personnes aiment les frites;
> deux personnes aiment la glace;
> deux personnes aiment le bœuf;
> une personne aime le poisson;
> et une personne aime les hamburgers.

Ecoute la cassette (6)

Les commandes

You are helping out in the kitchen. Your job is to note down customers' orders as they are shouted to you by the waiters through the door. To help, you have a copy of tonight's menu. Mark the table number beside each dish as it is ordered.

Un peu de lecture

Le menu du jour

An English customer has come into the restaurant. You are asked to explain to him what's on the menu tonight as he does not understand it at all. Note it all down in English in case you need to do it again.

HOTEL DE LA POSTE

Rue de la Vieille Poste
Châteauroux

Tél: 54 47 65 84

Menu à 150 francs

Hors d'oeuvres
Salade de tomates
Plat de crudités
Soupe à l'oignon
Escargots

Entrées
Filet de boeuf
Steak au poivre
Truite à l'amande

Garnis d'une sélection de légumes en saison

Sélection de fromage

Desserts

Melon surprise
Salade de fruits
Glaces – vanille – chocolat – pistache – fraise

Service 15% Compris

RESTAURANT OUVERT TOUS LES JOURS

Vocabulaire

agiter to shake	**gratter** to scrape/scratch
agneau (*m*) lamb	**griller** to grill
ail (*m*) garlic	**huile** (*f*) oil
ajouter to add	**huître** (*f*) oyster
armoire (*f*) tall cupboard	**jaune d'œuf** (*m*) yoke of egg
bœuf (*m*) beef	**lapin** (*m*) rabbit
bouillir to boil	**litre** (*m*) litre
canard (*m*) duck	**louche** (*f*) soup ladle
carte (*f*) card, menu	**maquereau** (*m*) mackerel
casserole (*f*) saucepan	**mijoter** to simmer
congélateur (*m*) freezer	**morceau** (*m*) piece, bit
couper to cut/slice	**morue** (*f*) cod
couteau (*m*) knife	**moule** (*f*) mussel
couvrir cover	**moutarde** (*f*) mustard
crabe (*f*) crab	**mouton** (*m*) mutton
crudités raw vegetables	**mélanger** to mix
cuillerée (*f*) spoonful	**œuf dur** (*m*) hard-boiled egg
cuillère à sauce (*f*) sauce spoon	**persil** (*m*) parsley
cuisinière (*f*) cooker	**pincée** (*f*) pinch
cuisses de grenouilles (*f*) frogs' legs	**placard** (*m*) cupboard
droite (*f*) right	**planche à hâcher** (*f*) chopping-board
eau (*f*) water	**poivre** (*m*) pepper
électrique electric	**poubelle** (*f*) rubbish bin
entrecôte (*m*) rib steak	**poulet** (*m*) chicken
éplucher to peel	**poêle** (*f*) frying-pan
escargot (*m*) snail	**raie** (*f*) skate
etagère (*f*) shelf	**râper** to grate
évier (*m*) sink	**recette** (*f*) recipe
faire cuire to cook	**remuer** to stir
faire frire to fry	**sardine** (*f*) sardine
farce (*f*) stuffing	**sel** (*m*) salt
fines herbes (*f*) herbs for seasoning	**sole** (*f*) sole
four (*m*) oven	**soupière** (*f*) soup tureen
frigo (*m*) fridge	**tablier** (*m*) apron
fruits de mer (*m*) sea food	**tire-bouchon** (*m*) corkscrew
garnir to garnish/decorate	**tiroir** (*m*) drawer
gauche (*f*) left	**tourner** to turn/mix
gaz (*m*) gas	**truite** (*f*) trout
gramme (*m*) gram	**vinaigre** (*m*) vinegar

Having worked in the kitchens of the Hôtel de la Poste you now have the opportunity to wait at table in both the café and the restaurant.

On sert à table

At the end of this unit you should be able to:

1 Understand and take down simple orders for food and drink and respond politely.
2 Order items of food and drink.
3 Read and understand a French menu.
4 Understand and explain what is in some common dishes.

Ecoute la cassette (1)

Il y a beaucoup de monde au café

Note down what each person wants to drink.

HOTEL DE LA POSTE

Rue de la Vieille Poste
Châteauroux

Tél: 54 47 65 84

RESTAURANT OUVERT TOUS LES JOURS

Sais-tu comprendre ce que demandent les clients?

Je voudrais . . .		
une bière	(pression)	
une glace	à la vanille à la fraise au chocolat au citron	
une tisane un Orangina un Perrier		

un café	noir crème au lait	
un chocolat	chaud froid	
un thé	au lait au citron	
un apéritif un whisky un cognac		
un vin	blanc rouge rosé	

. . . et sais-tu répondre?

Oui, Monsieur.
    Madame.
    Mademoiselle.

De suite!

Oui, Monsieur, j'arrive.

Vous désirez autre chose,
Monsieur/Madame?

Bien sûr, Monsieur.
    Madame.
    Mademoiselle.

Voilà, Monsieur.
    Madame.
    Mademoiselle.

Et maintenant à toi

Commander quelquechose!

Travaille avec ton collègue.

Turn over the cards and order your drink. Your partner will answer 'Oui Madame, Mademoiselle, Monsieur'.

Toi: Garçon, un Orangina, s'il vous plaît!
Ton collègue: Oui, Madame, de suite!

Changez de rôles et recommencez.

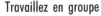
Travaillez en groupe

Vous êtes au café!

In a group of four or six make up a café scene in which you give orders for drinks. One of you is the waiter and the others are customers.

A vous tous

Café-théâtre

Act out the scene you have prepared for the rest of your class.
The others should note what you order and then tell the teacher/assistant.

Sais-tu comprendre les commandes?

Je voudrais une crêpe.
　　　　　un sandwich ⎰ au jambon.
　　　　　　　　　　　⎱ au fromage.
　　　　　　　　　　　⎱ au pâté.
　　　　　un croque-monsieur.
　　　　　des frites.

Sais-tu comprendre les questions?

Qu'est que vous avez comme sandwichs?

Qu'est que qu'il y a dans un croque-monsieur?

C'est combien, les frites?
　　　　　　　　les sandwichs?

. . . et sais-tu répondre?

Nous avons des sandwichs ⎰ au jambon.
　　　　　　　　　　　　⎱ au fromage.
　　　　　　　　　　　　⎱ au pâté.

Un croque-monsieur, c'est du pain grillé avec du jambon et du fromage.

Les frites, c'est 4f.20.
Les sandwichs au fromage, c'est 6f.

Vous avez choisi?

Ecoute la cassette (2)

On commande à boire et à manger

Note down each customer's order.

HOTEL DE LA POSTE

Rue de la Vieille Poste
Châteauroux

Tél: 54 47 65 84

Et maintenant à toi

Que désirez-vous?

Travaille avec ton collègue.

(A) **Le serveur/la serveuse**	**Le client/la cliente**
Say hello and ask what he/she wants . . .	
	Say you want a cheese sandwich and a beer.
Say of course, right away.	Ask how much that is.
Say it's 8f 50.	Say thank you very much.
(B) **Le serveur/la serveuse**	**Le client/la cliente**
Say hello and ask what he/she wants.	Say hello and ask what a croque-monsieur is.
Tell him/her.	Say you'll have a cheese sandwich.
Say OK and tell him/her that will be 6 francs. Ask if he/she wants anything else.	Say yes you'll have a coke.
Say of course, right away.	

Work through the two dialogues above and then make up your own.

Travaillez en groupe

Encore au café!

Make up another café scene. This time you can order food as well as drink. When you have prepared it you can act it for your friends.

A vous tous

Qu'est-ce qu'ils ont choisi?

Listen and note what each group orders. Be prepared to tell your teacher or the assistant, in French, what was asked for.

e.g. Cinq personnes ont choisi du vin rouge.
Trois personnes ont choisi des sandwichs au jambon.
Une personne a choisi une glace à la vanille.

Ecoute la cassette (3)

Au restaurant

Several groups of people arrive at the restaurant. Listen to what they say and note on a copy of this grid what is said.

	No. de personnes	Réservations	Table disponible	No. de Table
1				
2				
3				
4				
5				

Sais-tu accueillir des gens?

> Bonsoir, Messieurs Dames.
> Vous avez réservé?
> Vous avez fait une réservation?

Garçon!

. . . et sais-tu comprendre ce qu'on te demande?

> Vous avez de la place?

> Vous avez une table pour trois personnes?

> Vous avez une table de libre?

> Le menu, s'il vous plaît.

> La carte des vins, s'il vous plaît.

. . . et sais-tu répondre?

> Oui, par ici, s'il vous plaît.

> Non, je regrette.

> Oui, bien sûr.

> Voici le menu.

> Voici la carte des vins.

Et maintenant à toi

Vous avez réservé?

Travaille avec ton collègue.

(A) **Toi**	Ton collègue
Bonsoir, Monsieur, etc	Bonsoir. Vous avez une table pour quatre personnes?
Vous avez réservé?	Non, je regrette.
Ça va! Par ici, s'il vous plaît.	Merci.
(B) **Toi**	Ton collègue
Greet him/her.	Say good evening and ask if he/she has a table for five.
Ask if he/she has reserved a table.	Say yes you have.
Say very good, this way please.	Thank the waiter.

When you have practised the above roles make up your own dialogue.

Prends ton stylo

Les réservations

When you have repeated your dialogue to the teacher or assistant write it out as accurately as you can.

Ecoute la cassette (4)

Les clients commandent le repas

You have shown three customers to a table and given them the menu. Listen to what they want and mark it on a pad.

Sais-tu demander aux clients ce qu'ils désirent?

Bonjour!
Bonsoir, Messieurs Dames. Vous désirez?
Vous avez choisi?
Votre commande, s'il vous plaît?
Et ensuite?
Comme entrée, vous désirez?
Comme dessert, vous désirez?
Vous voulez la carte des vins?
Comme vin vous désirez?
Comment préférez-vous votre steak?

Sais-tu comprendre ce qu'ils commandent?

Pour commencer?

> Je voudrais du potage
> de la soupe   à l'oignon
>   de poisson
> du pâté (maison)
> des hors d'œuvres
> des crudités
> l'assiette de fruits de mer, s'il vous plaît.

Comme entrée?

un bifteck (hâché)	des carottes
un steak (bleu,	du chou
saignant, à point,	du chou-fleur
cuit, bien cuit)	des épinards
une côtelette (de porc,	des haricots
d'agneau, de veau)	des petits pois
du jambon	des pommes de terre
du poulet rôti	du riz
la selle d'agneau	des frites
du lapin	des pâtes
du porc	de la salade (verte,
	aux tomates)
la raie (au beurre noir)	
une omelette	
une quiche lorraine	
le plat du jour	

Comme dessert?

du fromage (au choix)	des fraises
du gâteau	des framboises
de la glace	des pêches
de la tarte	des poires
des fruits	des pommes
des abricots	des prunes
des bananes	du raisin
des cerises	

Prends ton stylo

On prépare un menu

Now plan your own menu. Use a word processor if you can.

Travaillez en groupe

On explique un menu

Give your menu to someone else and let them explain to a third person what is in it.

Et maintenant à toi

On commande à manger

Travaille avec ton collègue.

Read the menu and, taking it in turns to give and receive the order, decide what you want and order it. Don't forget to be very polite!

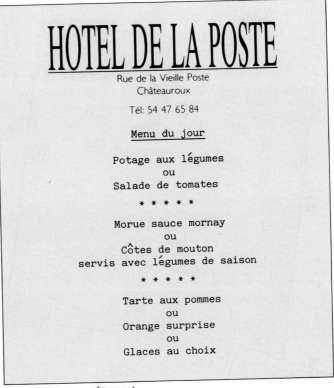

HOTEL DE LA POSTE

Rue de la Vieille Poste
Châteauroux

Tél: 54 47 65 84

Menu du jour

Potage aux légumes
ou
Salade de tomates

* * * * *

Morue sauce mornay
ou
Côtes de mouton
servis avec légumes de saison

* * * * *

Tarte aux pommes
ou
Orange surprise
ou
Glaces au choix

Et maintenant à toi

On sert à table

Travaille avec ton collègue.

One of you is the waiter/waitress, the other plays the part of the customer.

Toi: 1 Greet your customer politely.
2 Ask him/her what he/she wants.

Ton collègue: 1 Respond politely.
2 Turn over the cards and say you would like the item shown.

e.g. Je voudrais du poulet, s'il vous plait.

Changez de rôles.

Un peu de lecture

On aide des étrangers anglophones

One day a group of Americans arrive and they ask you to explain what is on the tourist menus. Work with a partner and take it in turns to explain what is on the various menus.

HOTEL DE LA POSTE

Rue de la Vieille Poste
Châteauroux

Tél: 54 47 65 84

Menu touristique à 65f

Potage du jour

Steak-frites

Fromage au choix

Fruits

HOTEL DE LA POSTE

Rue de la Vieille Poste
Châteauroux

Tél: 54 47 65 84

Menu touristique à 70f.

Pâté maison

Côtelette de porc
avec
Choix de légumes

Fromages au choix

Glaces au choix

HOTEL DE LA POSTE

Rue de la Vieille Poste
Châteauroux

Tél: 54 47 65 84

Menu touristique à 120f.

Hors d'oeuvres variés
ou
Assiette de fruits de mer
ou
Soupe de poisson

Raie au beurre noir
ou
Selle d'agneau
Avec choix de légumes en saison

Fromages

Gâteau au chocolat
ou
Fraises à la crème
ou
Choix de glaces ou sorbets

HOTEL DE LA POSTE

Rue de la Vieille Poste
Châteauroux

Tél: 54 47 65 84

Menu touristique à 75f.

Crudités ou
Potage du jour

Steak
ou
Côtes d'agneau
avec
Choix de légumes

Tarte aux prunes
ou
Glaces au choix

Sais-tu expliquer les plats?

mornay –	avec une sauce blanche dans laquelle il y a du gruyère râpé.
au gratin –	(un plat) couvert de gruyère râpé.
à la provençale –	avec une sauce de l'ail, des oignons et des tomates
salade niçoise –	du thon, des anchois, des haricots verts et des olives avec des tomates, des pommes de terre, etc.
chasseur –	une sauce avec des champignons et du vin.

Et maintenant à toi

On explique les plats

Travaille avec ton collègue.

Toi	Ton collègue
Bonjour, Madame, vous désirez?	Qu'est-ce que c'est, la soupe du jour?
C'est une soupe à l'oignon, Madame.	Très bien, alors, une soupe du jour. Et qu'est-ce que c'est, le poulet chasseur?
C'est du poulet avec une sauce aux champignons et au vin, Madame.	Bien, alors un poulet chasseur avec des haricots verts.
Say good evening and ask what s/he would like.	Ask what is in the soup of the day.
Say it's tomato soup.	Say fine, you'll have it. Ask what 'morue sauce mornay' is.
Tell her/him.	Say fine, you'll have it.

See if you can make up a dialogue like the two above.

Sais-tu servir le repas?

> **Voilà Monsieur, Madame, Mademoiselle. Ça va bien?**
> **Vous avez terminé?**

Sais-tu comprendre ce qui manque? . . . et sais-tu répondre?

> **S'il vous plaît, on peut avoir . . .**
>
> **de l'eau/du vin?**
> **de l'huile/du vinaigre?**
> **du sel/du poivre?**
> **du sucre?**
>
> **Il manque un couteau.**
> **une cuillère.**
> **une fourchette.**
> **une tasse.**
> **un verre.**

> **Mais oui, certainement.**
>
> **Je vais vous en chercher (un/une).**

Ecoute la cassette (5)

La soirée au restaurant

The head-waiter has asked you to listen as he greets and serves clients.
See if you can work out what is said.

1 How many people are in the party?
2 Have they reserved a table?
3 Where do they sit?
4 What do they choose for starters?
5 Which dish do they ask to be explained?
6 What main course(s) do they choose?
7 What dessert do they choose?
8 What else do they ask for?
9 What is missing from the table?
10 What else do they comment on?

Vocabulaire

accueillir to welcome, greet	**hors d'œuvre** (*m*) starter course
anchois (*m*) anchovy	**libre** free
banane (*f*) banana	**légume** (*m*) vegetable
bien cuit well cooked	**manquer** to miss
bière (*f*) beer	**pâté** (*m*) pâté, meat paste
blanc white	**pâtes** (*f*) pasta
bleu barely cooked (steak)	**place** (*f*) place or space/room
champignon (*m*) mushroom	**point: à point** medium (steak)
chaud hot	**poire** (*f*) pear
chercher to look for	**pomme** (*f*) apple
choisir to choose	**potage** (*m*) soup
choix (*m*) choice	**prune** (*f*) plum
chou (*m*) cabbage	**quiche lorraine** (*f*) cheese and
chou-fleur (*m*) cauliflower	bacon flan
citron (*m*) lemon	**raie** (*f*) **au beurre noir** skate
commande (*f*) order	cooked in brown butter sauce
commander to order	**raisin** (*m*) grape(s)
croque-monsieur (*m*) toasted	**repas** (*m*) meal
cheese and ham sandwich	**riz** (*m*) rice
crêpe (*f*) pancake	**rosé** pink (used of wine)
crudités (*f.pl*) raw vegetables	**rouge** red
cuit cooked	**réserver** to reserve
de suite right away	**râper** to grate
disponible available	**saignant** rare (of steak)
désirer to want	**salade** (*f*) salad
entrée (*f*) main course	**selle** (*f*) **d'agneau** saddle of lamb
épinards (*m*) spinach	**soupe** (*f*) soup
fraise (*f*) strawberry	**tasse** (*f*) cup
framboise (*f*) raspberry	**tisane** (*f*) herbal tea
froid cold	**thon** (*m*) tuna
fromage (*m*) cheese	**vanille** (*f*) vanilla
fruits de mer (*m.pl*) sea-food	**verre** (*m*) glass
gâteau (*m*) cake	**vin** (*m*) wine

UNITÉ 4

On fait le ménage

While you are working at the Hôtel de la Poste, Madam Cheritweitzer expects you to take your turn at cleaning and preparing rooms and helping guests.

At the end of this unit you should be able to:

1 Understand and give simple instructions regarding housework.
2 Understand requests from hotel guests and respond suitably and politely.
3 Report items requiring replacement or repair.
4 Give directions to guests about where various rooms are to be found in the hotel.

Ecoute la cassette (1)

Ce qu'il faut faire aujourd'hui

Each morning Mme Cheritweitzer gives you instructions as to what you have to do. Note down what you must do today.

Sais-tu parler du matériel de ménage?

un balai	broom	**le cire**	wax
un aspirateur	vacuum cleaner	**une bombe**	aerosol spray
une brosse	brush	**un seau**	bucket
une pelle	dustpan	**un fer à repasser**	iron
un torchon	duster	**une ampoule**	light bulb

Sais-tu parler du ménage?

S'il te plaît, S'il vous plaît,	fais faites }	les lits.
	passe passez }	l'aspirateur.
	nettoie nettoyez }	la salle de bain. la salle d'eau.
	range rangez }	les draps dans le placard.
	change changez }	le lit.
	cire cirez }	les meubles.
	balaie balayez }	l'entrée.
	mets mettez }	la machine à laver.
	nettoie nettoyez {	le palier. l'escalier. l'ascenseur. le couloir.
	lave lavez }	le plancher.
	vide videz }	la poubelle.

> Fais les lits!
> Passe l'aspirateur!
> Balaie l'entrée!
> Nettoie la salle de bain!

Et maintenant à toi

Tu donnes des ordres

There is a young French boy, Pierre-Jean, who is doing odd jobs at the hotel during his holiday. Today he is working with you. Give him instructions using the **tu** form.

Travaille avec ton collègue.

> **e.g.**   **Toi:**   Change le lit, s'il te plaît.
> **Ton collègue:**   Oui, très bien.

Changez de rôles.

Ecoute la cassette (2)

Organiser sa journée

Note down what you are told to do and then put the jobs in the order in which you intend to do them.

Qu'est-ce que tu vas faire?

Et maintenant à toi

Now read out the list to your partner.

> **e.g.** D'abord, je vais changer les lits.
> Puis, je vais mettre la machine à laver.
> Puis, je vais cirer les meubles.

Sais-tu ce qu'il y a dans une chambre?

une table de nuit	et sur le lit:
une armoire	une couverture
une chaise	un matelas
un fauteuil	un oreiller
un lit	un drap
les rideaux	une taie d'oreiller
un tapis	
une étagère	
une poubelle	
une lampe	
un cintre	

. . . et dans la salle de bains?

une baignoire	un W.C.
une douche	une serviette
un lavabo	un gant de toilette
une prise-rasoir	du savon
du papier hygiénique	du shampooing
un bidet	un robinet

Ecoute la cassette (3)

Les demandes des clients

While you are carrying out your tasks one day several guests ask you for different items. Note down what is required in each room.

HOTEL DE LA POSTE

Rue de la Vieille Poste
Châteauroux

Tél: 54 47 65 84

RESTAURANT OUVERT TOUS LES JOURS

Et maintenant à toi

Il me faut . . .

You, in your turn, have to go and ask Mme Cheritzweitzer for what is required. Work with your partner and take it in turns.

> **e.g.** Du savon pour la chambre numéro 7, s'il vous plaît.
> Des serviettes pour la chambre numéro 3, s'il vous plaît.

Sais-tu comprendre ce qui ne va pas? . . . et sais-tu répondre poliment?

Ce qui ne va pas

Working with your partner, take turns to lift a card and say what is wrong. The other person answers appropriately.

e.g. Il n'y a pas de savon.
Je vais en chercher.

Sais-tu ce qu'il y a dans le salon?

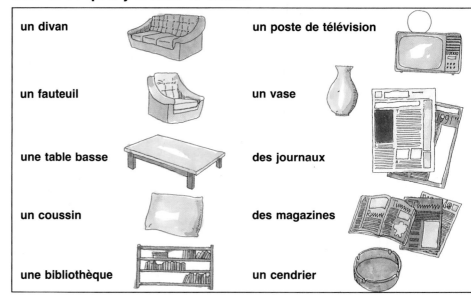

un divan

un fauteuil

une table basse

un coussin

une bibliothèque

un poste de télévision

un vase

des journaux

des magazines

un cendrier

Ecoute la cassette (4)

Encore du travail

Mme Cheritweitzer asks you to do some more jobs. Note down what you are asked to do.

Prends ton stylo

Fais la liste

You are asked to make a list in French of 10 of your daily tasks! You can then decide which you will do and which you will delegate to someone else.

Et maintenant à toi

Division du travail

You have your young helper, Pierre-Jean, with you again. Using the list you have written, tell him what you are going to do and what you would like him to do.

Travaille avec ton collègue.

e.g. **Toi:** Moi, je lave le plancher. Toi, tu nettoies l'ascenseur.
Ton collègue: Oui, d'accord.

Sais-tu expliquer où se trouvent les pièces de l'hôtel?

à droite	la première porte à droite
à gauche	la deuxième porte à gauche
	tout de suite à gauche après le restaurant
tout droit	tout droit au bout du couloir

Et maintenant à toi

Où se trouve . . .?

Travaille avec ton collègue.

Toi	Ton collègue
Où se trouve le téléphone, s'il vous plaît?	A droite après le restaurant.
Merci beaucoup.	De rien.

Toi	Ton collègue
Ask where the toilets are.	At the end of the corridor on the left.
Say thank you.	Say don't mention it.

Now make up some dialogues of your own.

Vocabulaire

ampoule (f)	light bulb		**journal** (m)	newspaper
armoire (f)	cupboard		**lampe** (f)	lamp
ascenseur (m)	lift		**lavabo** (m)	wash-basin
aspirateur (m)	vacuum-cleaner		**machine à laver** (f)	washing-machine
baignoire (f)	bath		**matelas** (m)	mattress
balai (m)	broom		**mettre**	to put, to put on
balayer	to sweep		**meubles** (m)	furniture
bas, basse	low		**ménage** (m)	housework
bibliothèque (f)	bookcase		**nettoyer**	to clean
bidet (m)	bidet		**oreiller** (m)	pillow
bombe (f)	aerosol spray		**palier** (m)	landing
bout: au bout de	at the end of		**papier hygiénique** (m)	toilet-paper
brosse (f)	brush		**passer**	to pass
casser	to break		**pelle** (f)	dustpan
cendrier (m)	ashtray		**plancher** (m)	floor
chaise (f)	chair		**poste de télévision** (m)	T.V. set
changer	to change		**poubelle** (f)	rubbish-bin
cintre (m)	coathanger		**prise-rasoir** (f)	razor socket
cire (m)	polish		**ranger**	to put away
cirer	to wax, to polish		**rideau** (m)	curtain
couler	to run, leak		**robinet** (m)	tap
couloir (m)	corridor		**sale**	dirty
coussin (m)	cushion		**salle d'eau** (f)	shower room
couverture (m)	blanket		**savon** (m)	soap
divan (m)	divan bed, sofa		**seau** (f)	bucket
douche (f)	shower		**serviette** (f)	towel
drap (m)	sheet		**shampooing** (m)	shampoo
droit: tout droit	straight on		**table de nuit** (f)	bedside table
droite: à droite	on the right		**taie d'oreiller** (f)	pillowcase
entrée (f)	entrance hall		**tapis** (m)	rug
escalier (m)	staircase		**toilette** (f)	toilet
fer à repasser (m)	iron		**torchon** (m)	duster
fermer	to close		**vase** (m)	vase
gant de toilette (m)	flannel, face-cloth		**vider**	to empty
gauche: à gauche	on the left			

UNITÉ 5

A la réception de l'hôtel

To complete your work experience in the Hôtel de la Poste, you are now helping at the reception desk.

At the end of this unit you should be able to:

1 Understand and give directions.
2 Describe hotel accommodation.
3 Take reservations.
4 Order taxis and take reservations by telephone.

Ecoute la cassette (1)

Pour aller à . . .?

One morning, some of the hotel guests are asking M. Cheritweitzer their way around. When he replies, follow on the map the way that people must go, so that you will be able to answer such questions.

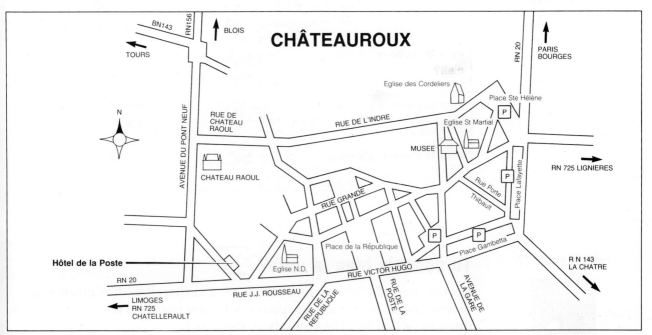

Sais-tu indiquer le chemin?

Pour le syndicat d'initiative, s'il vous plaît?
Pour l'église, s'il vous plaît?

Tournez à gauche.

Pour les toilettes, s'il vous plaît?
Pour le stade, s'il vous plaît?

Tournez à droite.

Pour le marché, s'il vous plaît?

Allez tout droit.

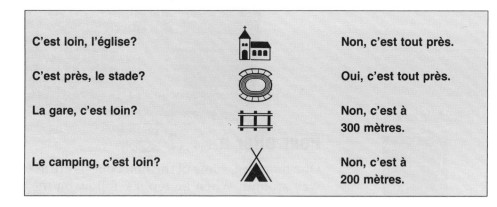

C'est loin, l'église?

Non, c'est tout près.

C'est près, le stade?

Oui, c'est tout près.

La gare, c'est loin?

Non, c'est à 300 mètres.

Le camping, c'est loin?

Non, c'est à 200 mètres.

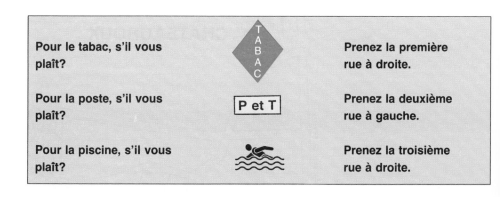

Pour le tabac, s'il vous plaît?

Prenez la première rue à droite.

Pour la poste, s'il vous plaît?

Prenez la deuxième rue à gauche.

Pour la piscine, s'il vous plaît?

Prenez la troisième rue à droite.

Ecoute la cassette (2)

Tu connais bien la ville?

On the map of Châteauroux which M. Cheritweitzer has given you, several places which guests often ask for are not marked. Can you mark them in, when he tells you where they are?

Le plan du quartier

Your teacher will give you a blank plan and a list of places which you must find. Your partner will have a map similar to the one below with places marked. By asking where these places are, you will be able to complete your plan.

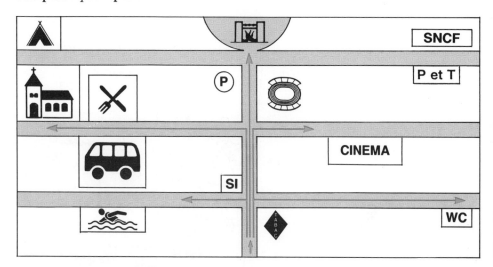

Now swap roles, using different plans.

Sais-tu dire où se trouvent . . .?

le musée les toilettes le château la piscine l'église la poste	.... à gauche de l'hôtel de ville. .... à droite du tabac. .... en face de l'hôtel de ville.
le cabinet du dentiste le cabinet du médecin	
	.... à côté du supermarché.
un coiffeur un bureau de renseignements un tabac un kiosque à journaux une pharmacie une banque	.... près du parking. .... pas loin du stade. .... au coin de la rue.
.... et te rappelles-tu de 'devant' et 'derrière'?	

C'est où exactement?

Add five more places to the plan you have already used. Tell your partner what they are, and answer his/her question about exactly where they are.

e.g. C'est où exactement la piscine?

Dans la deuxième rue à gauche. A côté de l'église.

Un peu de lecture

Le mot de l'architecte

M. Cheritweitzer has received this note from his friend, the Town Architect, giving him advance warning of proposed major changes to the town centre. He asks you to mark them on a map for him, to give him a better idea of what effect these proposals will have.

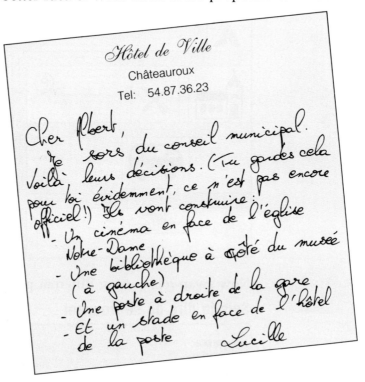

Sais-tu parler de l'hébergement offert par un hôtel?

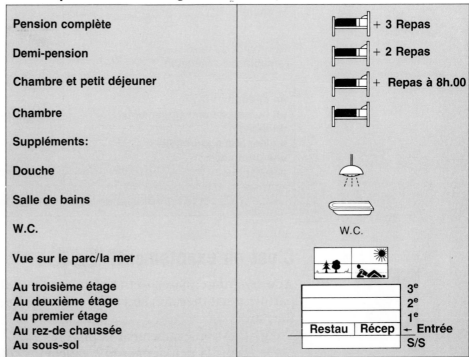

Pension complète	+ 3 Repas
Demi-pension	+ 2 Repas
Chambre et petit déjeuner	+ Repas à 8h.00
Chambre	
Suppléments:	
Douche	
Salle de bains	
W.C.	W.C.
Vue sur le parc/la mer	
Au troisième étage	3ᵉ
Au deuxième étage	2ᵉ
Au premier étage	1ᵉ
Au rez-de chaussée	Restau Récep ← Entrée
Au sous-sol	S/S

Ecoute la cassette (3)

Qu'est-ce qu'il y a comme chambres?

Mme Cheritweitzer takes you on a tour of the hotel to show you the facilities in the different rooms.

Make a note of the room numbers according to the type of room.

e.g. Chambres avec lavabo (une ou deux personnes): numéros 205, . . .

Travaillez en groupe

C'est quoi comme chambre?

M. Cheritweitzer has asked you to learn which room has which facilities. Work in a group of four or five. One of you should call out the room number, and the others try to reply as quickly as possible with its description, using the information you noted down in the last exercise.

e.g. Chambre numéro 210!
Chambre avec douche et W.C., pour une ou deux personnes!

Sais-tu comprendre ce que demandent les clients?

> **Vous avez des chambres de libre?**
>
> **Vous faites pension complète?**
>
> **Je voudrais une chambre pour deux personnes.**
>
> **Je voudrais une chambre avec salle de bains.**
>
> **Le petit déjeuner est compris?**

. . . et sais-tu donner et demander les renseignements nécessaires?

> **Oui, nous avons des chambres de libre.**
> **Non, nous sommes complets.**
>
> **Vous êtes combien?**
>
> **C'est pour ce soir uniquement?**
>
> **Vous restez combien de nuits?**
>
> **Vous voulez une chambre avec douche?**
>   **salle de bains?**
>   **vue sur le parc?**
>
> **Vous prenez le petit déjeuner?**
>   **la pension complète?**
>
> **Je vous donne la chambre 205.**
>
> **Voilà la clef, Monsieur/Madame.**

Ecoute la cassette (4)

Tu marques les réservations

You are helping M. Cheritweitzer on the reception desk. While he talks to clients as they arrive to check in, he asks you to fill in the booking form.

HOTEL DE LA POSTE

Rue de la Vieille Poste
Châteauroux

Tél: 54 47 65 84

Date	Client(s)	Chambre No.	Nuits	Pension/Demi-Pension

Et maintenant à toi

Tu fais des réservations

Travaille avec ton collègue.

(A) Le receptionniste	Le client
Bonjour, Monsieur/Madame.	
	Vous avez des chambres de libre?
Oui, Monsieur/Madame. C'est pour combien de nuits?	
	C'est pour trois nuits.
Et vous êtes combien?	
	Je voudrais une chambre pour deux personnes.
Très bien. En pension complète?	
	Non, en demi-pension, s'il vous plaît.
Alors, je vous donne la chambre 207.	
	Merci.
(B) Le receptionniste	**Le client**
Say hello.	
	Ask if there are any vacant rooms.
Say that there are, and ask how many people this is for.	
	Say it's for 3 people, and that it's for 2 nights.
Say that's fine, and ask if full-board is required.	
	Say yes, please.
Say that they can have Room 211.	
	Say thank you.

Travaillez en groupe

Réserver une chambre

Look carefully at this plan which shows six possible hotel-room bookings. Then throw the dice in turn. After each throw of the dice, the thrower must 'book' the room which has that number. The player to his/her right will play the role of the receptionist.

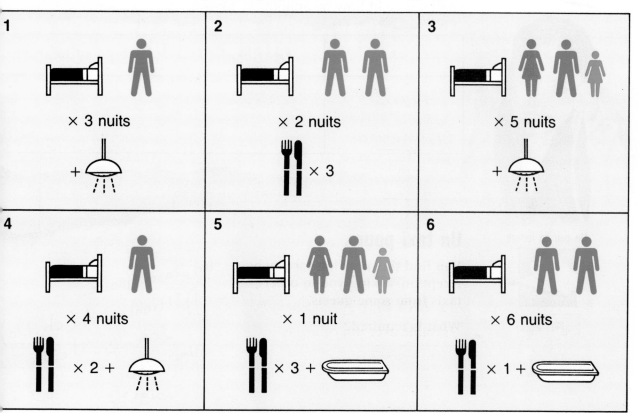

1 × 3 nuits + 🚿	**2** × 2 nuits 🍴 × 3	**3** × 5 nuits + 🚿
4 × 4 nuits 🍴 × 2 + 🚿	**5** × 1 nuit 🍴 × 3 + 🍽	**6** × 6 nuits 🍴 × 1 + 🍽

Sais-tu t'occuper des taxis . . .?

. . . en comprenant les clients de l'hôtel?

> Je peux commander un taxi d'ici?
> Un taxi pour 8h00, c'est possible?

. . . en précisant les détails?

> Oui, bien sûr. (Ici, tout est possible!)
> C'est pour quelle heure?
> Où voulez-vous aller?
> C'est au nom de Monsieur/Madame . . .

. . . en parlant au téléphone avec l'entreprise de taxis?

> Allô, ici l'Hôtel de la Poste.
> 'Georges' à l'appareil.
> Un taxi à 8h00, s'il vous plaît.
> Pour aller à . . .
> Au nom de Monsieur/Madame . . .

Ecoute la cassette (5)

Je vous écoute

M. Cheritweitzer wants you to get used to using the phone. He asks you to listen in on the **écouteur**, one afternoon, when a couple of guests ask him to order taxis. He asks you to note down at what time the taxis are required, and where the guests are going. He also tells you to take special note of how he announces himself on the phone.

	1er Client	2e Client
Heure Destination		

Un peu de lecture

Un taxi pour . . .

You find this note left for you at reception, asking you to order taxis from some guests.

What is required?

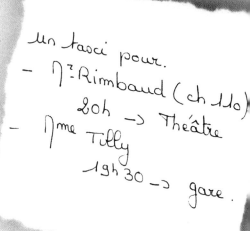

Un taxi pour.
- M. Rimbaud (ch 110)
  20h → Théâtre
- Mme Tilly
  19h30 → gare.

Et maintenant à toi

Commander un taxi

Travaille avec ton collègue.

Toi	Ton collègue
Allô, ici taxis Dunon.	Say who and where you are, and ask for a taxi at 8h00.
Où voulez-vous aller?	Say it's to go to the theatre.
Et c'est à quel nom?	Say it's for a M. Rimbaud.
C'est fait.	Say thanks and goodbye.

Now change roles, and order the taxi for Mme Tilly. (You have the information from the last exercise.) Now make up some similar conversations and practise them.

Sais-tu t'annoncer au téléphone?

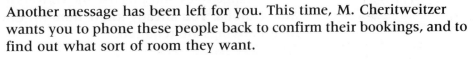

Allô, ici l'Hôtel de la Poste.
Jim Brown à l'appareil.
Je suis bien chez Monsieur/Madame . . .?

Ecoute la cassette (6)

Allô! L'Hôtel de la Poste

M. Cheritweitzer is busy on the phone. Again, he passes you the **écouteur**, and asks you to note down what each of the six conversations is about.

Un peu de lecture

Le mot de M. Cheritweitzer

Another message has been left for you. This time, M. Cheritweitzer wants you to phone these people back to confirm their bookings, and to find out what sort of room they want.

What does he want to know?
When do the guests want the rooms?

HOTEL DE LA POSTE
Rue de la Vieille Poste
Châteauroux
Tél: 54 47 65·84

Appelez pour confirmation
(chambre avec ou sans douche
salle de bains ou pas ?)

Mme Dutron   Mardi soir   78.66.32.40
    Lucan   Jeudi / Vendredi 37.42.31.00
Mme Gulutta Vendredi / Samedi 43.22.10.43.

RESTAURANT OUVERT TOUS LES JOURS

Confirmer les détails

Travaille avec ton collègue.

Toi	Ton collègue
Announce yourself, and ask if you are speaking to Mme Dutrou.	
	Oui, c'est bien Mme Dutrou.
Tell her that her room is reserved for Tuesday.	
	Très bien.
Ask if she wants a room with a shower or a bathroom.	
	Avec salle de bains, s'il vous plaît.
Thank her and say you will see her on Tuesday.	
	A mardi, au revoir.

Then change roles and practise the conversations about M. Lucan and Mlle Oululla. You already know from M. Cheritweitzer's note when their bookings are required.

La confirmation pour M. Cheritweitzer

Write a note for M. Cheritweitzer, confirming the bookings and saying what sort of room each of the three requires.

e.g. Dutrou − confirmé − salle de bains

Vocabulaire

à côté de beside, next to
à l'appareil on the phone
allô hello (used only on the telephone)
au coin de on the corner of
banque (f) bank
bureau de renseignements (m) information office
cabinet du dentiste (m) dental surgery
cabinet du médecin (m) doctor's surgery
château (m) castle
clef (f) key
coiffeur (m) hairdresser
compris included in the price
confirmer to confirm
demi-pension (f) half board
derrière behind
devant in front of
douche (f) shower
droite right
écouteur (m) telephone ear-piece
église (f) church
en face de opposite

étage (m) floor/storey
gare (f) station
hébergement (m) accommodation
kiosque à journaux (m) newspaper booth
libre free
loin far
musée (m) museum
parc (m) park/gardens
pension complète (f) full board
pharmacie (f) chemist's shop
piscine (f) swimming pool
poste (f) post office
près near
rez de chaussée (m) ground floor
rue (f) street
sous-sol (m) basement
stade (m) stadium
supplément (m) extras
syndicat d'initiative (m) tourist office
tabac (m) tobacconist's shop
tout droit straight on
troisième third
vue (f) view

3 TROISIÈME PARTIE

Le Tourisme

In this section you will gain experience in the tourist industry. Initially you have a job in the town-twinning office of your local Town Hall. You then go with your group to your twin town in France, Onzain, where you act as a courier. Finally you spend some time working in the tourist office at Onzain.

UNITÉ 1

On s'occupe des visiteurs

While working in your Town Hall, you are asked to make or check the arrangements concerning travel and accommodation for several groups of French people who want to visit the town.

At the end of this unit you should be able to:

1 Describe simple arrangements regarding travel.
2 Understand and use the 24-hour clock.
3 Understand foreign visitors' travel requirements.
4 Describe simple future events.

Ecoute la cassette (1)

On arrive comment?

Listen as these people tell you how they intend to travel. See if you can link the numbers on the cassette with the pictures below.

a

b

c

d

e

Sais-tu dire comment tu voyages?

par le hovercraft	en auto/en voiture	en auto-stop
par le bateau	en autobus	à bicyclette
par le car-ferry	en avion	à vélo
par le métro	en hélicoptère	à moto
par le train	en taxi	à pied

Et maintenant à toi

Comment arrives-tu?

Travaille avec ton collègue.

Using these pictures to prompt you, tell your partner how you intend to travel on holiday.

> **e.g.** Comment arrives-tu?
>   J'arrive par le train.

Changez de rôles.

Sais-tu lire les horaires?

If you are going to make travel arrangements, you will need to be able to use the 24-hour clock, as most timetables are written using it.

e.g. 7.30 is 7.30 in the morning.
19.30 is 7.30 in the evening.
1.45 is 1.45 in the (very early) morning.
13.45 is 1.45 in the afternoon.

```
 7:30
```
```
19:30
```

Obviously, it is very important for a traveller to know if the times given are morning or afternoon, so when giving travel arrangements always use the 24-hour system, or specify whether you mean '**du matin**', '**de l'après-midi**' or '**du soir**'.

Un peu de lecture

L'horaire des trains

A group of English people are planning to go to St. Étienne to watch a football match. As they are travelling by train, and cannot make sense of the timetable, they ask you for help.

They intend to catch the train in Lille. See if you can answer their questions about the timetable.

19

LILLE - LYON - (ST-ÉTIENNE)

TGV n° (●) Note à consulter		510 1.2.	617 2.3.	617 2.4.	518 1.5.★	621 ★	627 6.★	627 7.★	512 1.8.	631 7.9.★
LILLE	🚗D	7.23	8.22	8.30	9.00	10.00	11.52	12.00	14.01	13.55
DOUAI	🚗D	7.42	8.44	8.52	9.19	10.19	12.12	12.21	14.21	14.17
ARRAS	🚗D	7.56	9.01	9.09	9.34	10.40	12.27	12.37	14.36	14.33
AMIENS	🚗D	*8.12*	*9.28*	*9.33*	*9.49*	*11.00*	*12.48*	13.18	*14.51*	15.16
LONGUEAU	D	8.27	9.40	9.46	10.05	11.12	12.58	I	15.07	I
PARIS Nord	🚗A	I	10.40	10.44	I	12.12	13.55	14.30	I	16.23
PARIS Lyon	🚗D		12.00	12.00		13.00	15.00	15.00		17.00
LYON Part-Dieu	🚗A	11.52	14.00	14.00	13.26	15.08	17.00	17.00	18.31	19.04
LYON Perrache	🚗A	12.02	14.10	14.10	13.36	15.18	17.10	17.10	18.41	19.14
ST-ÉTIENNE Châtx 🚗A		*13.13*	*15.13*	*15.13*	*15.13*	15.53	*18.17*	*18.17*	*19.53*	*20.19*

TGV n° (●) Note à consulter		831 2.	631 2.	639/659 ★	643 6.★	643 7.8.★	647 6.10.★	647 11.★	649 9.★	
LILLE	🚗D	14.00	14.00	16.00	17.00	17.00	18.03	18.06	19.00	
DOUAI	🚗D	14.22	14.22	16.22	17.23	17.23	18.22	18.28	19.21	
ARRAS	🚗D	14.39	14.39	16.39	17.44	17.44	18.37	18.44	19.37	
AMIENS	🚗D	—	—	—	—	18.24	—	*19.13*	*19.55*	
LONGUEAU	D	15.15	15.15	I	I	I	I	19.24	20.10	
PARIS Nord	🚗A	16.18	16.18	18.09	19.14	19.26	20.02	20.28	21.09	
PARIS Lyon	🚗D	16.49	17.00	19.00	20.00	20.00	21.00	21.00	21.50	
LYON Part-Dieu	🚗A	18.57	19.04	21.10	22.00	22.00	23.04	23.04	23.50	
LYON Perrache	🚗A	—	19.14	21.20	22.12	22.12	23.14	23.14	0.00	
ST-ÉTIENNE Châtx 🚗A		—	*20.19*	21.55	*23.15*	*23.28*	*0.23*	*0.23*	*1.00*	

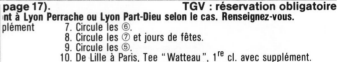

... page 17).   **TGV : réservation obligatoire**
... à Lyon Perrache ou Lyon Part-Dieu selon le cas. Renseignez-vous.
...plément   7. Circule les ⑥.
                             8. Circule les ⑦ et jours de fêtes.
                             9. Circule les ⑤.
                            10. De Lille à Paris, Tee "Watteau", 1re cl. avec supplément.
                                La correspondance pour St-Etienne n'a pas lieu les ⑤.
...u 09/04.   11. Ne circule pas les ⑥. Correspondance pour St-Etienne arr. 0.23
                                les ①, ②, ③ et ④ et arr. 1.00 les ⑦/①.

1 We should be in Lille by about 7.30 a.m. When is the first train for St. Étienne?
2 If we get that train, does it stop in Paris?
3 We would like to stop for a little sightseeing in Paris. If we stopped for three hours what would be the next train we could get after that?
4 We need to be in St. Étienne for an 8 p.m. kick-off. Will we arrive in time?
5 What is the latest train we could get from Lille that would get us to St. Étienne before 7 p.m.?

Ecoute la cassette (2)

Quelle heure est-il?

Listen to these people saying the time using the 24-hour clock. As you listen, make a note of the times, and say whether each refers to the morning, afternoon or evening.

e.g. Il est treize heures   (afternoon)

Et maintenant à toi

L'heure

Say these times to your partner, and ask him/her to write them down using the 24-hour clock.

e.g. dix heures du soir 22.00

1 sept heures du matin
2 huit heures du soir
3 neuf heures et demie du matin
4 une heure et quart de l'après-midi
5 trois heures du matin
6 midi et quart
7 minuit et demie
8 deux heures dix de l'après-midi
9 onze heures vingt-cinq du soir
10 onze heures vingt du matin

Ecoute la cassette (3)

Nous arrivons à...

The answering machine in your office has been very busy during the lunch hour! Some people for whom you have arranged a visit have phoned you to let you know at what time they will arrive in town so that you can let the hotels know when to expect them. You already know the names of the callers. Note in your book the time of each arrival, and the method of transport he or she intends to use. Make a copy of this grid in your book.

Nom	L'heure d'arrivée	Transport
M. Duclos		
Mme Petit		
M. Philippe		
Mme Blanc		
M. Fleur		

Et maintenant à toi

Les excursions

Here is some information about some of the more popular visits you are likely to be asked about. Take turns with your partner to play the role of the foreign visitor who is seeking information and the role of the clerk who answers the inquiries.

Destination	Method of Transport	Return Fares
London	**train:** every hour from 06.45 **bus:** twice a day 06.30, 15.45 **air:** one flight a day 07.15	£25.00 £12.50 £76.00
Stratford	**bus:** Saturdays 09.00, 12.00 daily 06.45, 08.45, 12.45 no service Sundays	£12.00 £10.00
Blackpool	**coach:** service Sat. and Sun departs 8.00 returns 23.45	£9.45

N.B. **toutes les heures** every hour; **deux fois par jour** twice a day; **la livre** pound.

Work through the dialogue below until you are confident, then make up some variations of your own:

Toi	Ton collègue
Bonjour, Madame/Monsieur.	
	Bonjour, je peux vous aider?
Oui, je voudrais visiter Blackpool, c'est possible?	
	Oui Madame/Monsieur. Il y a un car tous les samedis qui part à huit heures du matin.
Et ça coûte combien?	
Merci bien, Madame/Monsieur. Au revoir.	Ça coûte neuf livres quarante-cinq aller et retour, Madame/Monsieur.
	Au revoir, Madame/Monsieur. Bon voyage!

Sais-tu parler du futur?

Je vais	**arriver à neuf heures.**
Tu vas	**visiter en été.**
Il va	**prendre le train.**
Elle va	**réserver la chambre.**
Nous allons	**acheter le billet de train.**
Vous allez	**faire le voyage en bateau.**
Ils vont	**louer une voiture chez Hertz.**
Elles vont	**parler à M. le Maire.**

Un peu de lecture

Les profs. d'Onzain

Your office has received the fax shown opposite from a group of French teachers who are coming to England as part of the twinning arrangement your town has with Onzain. Note down the information given, so that the right arrangements can be made.

```
Monsieur,

        Nous allons arriver le jeudi 9 mai à vingt heures.
        Nous allons prendre le bateau et le train
        Réservez quatre chambres avec douche dans l'hôtel
        Vous   allez   organiser  une visite pour  le weekend?
        Nous allons passer le dimanche à Londres.
        M. Dutrac va prendre l'avion. Il va arriver mercredi
        à deux heures du matin.
        Il va loger avec un ami. Pas besoin d'hôtel.

                                            Merci


        Groupe de professeurs d'Onzain.
```

Ecoute la cassette (4)

On se déplace comment?

Listen as these people tell you how they intend to travel. Which form of transport is mentioned for each destination? Draw up two columns in your book, as below, and see if you can link each method of transport with the correct destination.

train

bateau

avion

voiture

à pied

musée

Glasgow

Douvres

Manchester

Irelande

Prends ton stylo

La délégation municipale

The Town Clerk has given you some details about a small group of the Mayor's staff who are planning a visit to Onzain. He asks you to write a short memo for him to fax in advance to Onzain, to prevent any confusion. Prepare it on a word processor if possible.

```
Mr Jones and five other people will arrive on Monday at 2 p.m.
They will travel by car.
They will eat at the hotel.
Reserve 1 double and 3 single rooms with showers, please.
Organise a visit to the Town Hall on Tuesday morning at
9.30 a.m., please.
```

Ecoute la cassette (5)

Vous êtes combien?

You have been asked to wait for a phone call from a member of a group which is to arrive next week from your twin town. The office already know what type of accommodation is required, but need to know the number involved, so as to make the proper arrangements. Make a copy of this grid and fill in the numbers.

Hébergement	Nombre
Camping	
Hôtel	
Chez des amis	
Auberge de Jeunesse	
Cité Universitaire	

Un peu de lecture

La lettre de M. Lemercier

Your office has received the following letter from France.

Lyon le 20 novembre.

Monsieur,

On m'a donné votre adresse au syndicat d'initiative.

J'ai l'intention de passer huit jours dans votre ville à partir du deux janvier de l'année prochaine.

Je vais arriver par le train de deux heures du matin.

Serait-il possible que l'on vienne me chercher à la gare? Pouvez-vous aussi me trouver un hôtel?

Comme je ne suis pas très riche, je voudrais un hôtel pas trop cher, disons £15 la nuit, c'est possible?

Merci par avance de votre gentillesse

Avec mes meilleurs sentiments

JC Lemercier

As the person responsible you are asked to write notes on what the letter is about. Make your notes under these headings.

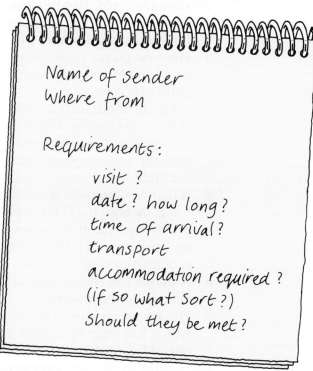

Name of sender
Where from

Requirements:

visit?
date? how long?
time of arrival?
transport
accommodation required?
(if so what sort?)
should they be met?

Et maintenant à toi

Pour aller à…?

You will need to be able to help people find their way around your town. Work through this dialogue with your partner.

Toi	Ton collègue
Bonjour, Monsieur/Madame.	Say hello.
Pour aller à la gare, c'est loin?	No, its not far, turn left at the door and walk 200 metres. Take the first left and the station is on the right.
Il y a un train pour Birmingham?	Yes, there's one at 14.00.
Merci bien, au revoir.	Not at all, goodbye.

Travaillez en groupe

Jeu de voyages

This is a game which practises forms of transport and times of day. There are three sets of ten different cards. One is a transport set and gives ten different forms of transport, one is a time set and gives ten different times of day, and one is a combined time and transport set (**carte de voyages**) which offers ten forms of transport with a particular time marked on each card. The aim of the game is to collect as many of these **cartes de voyages** as possible. Read the instructions on the next page.

1 Get into groups of three.
2 One member is the 'travel agent' and holds all the **cartes de voyages** cards. He/she deals an equal number of both the other sets of cards to the other members of the group. The rest of the cards are placed in two piles face down on the table.
3 The first player puts one time card and one transport card face up on the table and asks for that particular form of transport at that particular time.
  e.g. Je voudrais le bateau de sept heures.
4 If the 'travel agent' has that particular combination on a **carte de voyages** card, he/she hands it over to the player who keeps it and puts the separate time and transport cards back into the pile on the table.
5 If that combination is not available, the 'travel agent' has to say:
  e.g. Je regrette, il n'y a pas de bateau à sept heures.
  or   Je regrette, il n'y a pas de bateau.
  By listening carefully it will be possible to pick up clues as to what combinations are available.
6 A player can change one of his cards for one out of the pile on the table if he/she wishes.
7 The turn then passes to the next player who may pick up the card which has been discarded provided that he in turn throws down one of his cards.
The winner is the first person to have no cards to play. He/she will be left with only **carte de voyages** cards.

Ecoute la cassette (6)

Des renseignements

There are a number of enquiries waiting on your answering machine from various French people. Make a note in your book of what each person wants to know, so that you can call them back with the answer.

Vocabulaire

acheter	to buy	**matin** (*m*)	morning
après-midi (*m*)	afternoon	**moto(cyclette)** (*f*)	motorbike
arriver	to arrive	**métro** (*m*)	underground railway
auto (*f*)	car	**nuit** (*f*)	night
auto-stop (*m*)	hitch-hiking	**parler**	to talk
autobus (*m*)	bus	**pied** (*m*)	foot
avion (*m*)	plane	**prendre**	to take
bateau (*m*)	boat	**regretter**	to be sorry
bicyclette (*f*)	bike	**renseignement** (*m*)	information
billet (*m*)	ticket	**se déplacer**	to move around
car-ferry (*m*)	car ferry	**soir** (*m*)	evening
chez	at the home of	**taxi** (*m*)	taxi
fois: une fois once; **deux fois**	twice	**tout, tous, toutes**	every
hovercraft (*m*)	hovercraft	**train** (*m*)	train
hélicoptère (*m*)	helicopter	**visiter**	to visit
louer	to hire, rent	**voyage** (*m*)	journey
maire (*m*)	mayor	**vélo** (*m*)	bike

UNITÉ 2

Accompagnateur de groupe

This unit is about the second stage of your job with the twinning office. It takes place in Onzain, the twin town in the Loire Valley. You will be acting as courier for the English group that is due to stay in Onzain for the twinning anniversary celebrations. You will be working closely with François, who is a clerk in the Town Hall in Onzain.

At the end of this unit you should be able to :

1 Ask for and reserve different types of accommodation.
2 Understand and explain details of local transport facilities.
3 Understand and explain details of local events/entertainments.
4 Arrange excursions.
5 Report losses and thefts.

Ecoute la cassette (1)

L'hébergement

François explains for you the range of hotels and other types of accommodation which Onzain has. Can you make a list of the ones he mentions? Some of them are advertised below and opposite.

A proximité de la forêt et de la rivière Ancienne propriété du Baron de Coubertin Sol herbeux et plat

CAMPING LES AMIS DE LA NATURE***

CISO

Centre International de Séjour d'Onzain

46 Avenue de la République
41150 Onzain Tél: 54 73 14 22
(Près de la gare SNCF)

TARIFS GROUPES 1990

HEBERGEMENT :
- Par personne et par nuit, petit déjeuner compris. Chambre avec lavabo, douche, table et chaise.

Chambre à 1 lit	86 FF
Chambre à 2 lits	67 FF
Chambre à 3 lits	57 FF
Chambre à 4 lits	53 FF

GITES RURAUX

MONTEAUX

Mme Bonamy Alice,
route de Cangey, Monteaux,
41150 Onzain   tél. 54 70 25 16

Sem: HS 926F BS 845 F WE 358 F
Pers. suppl.: 15F par jour
Jours suppl.: 120F
Réservation: S.R.

CHOUZY s/Cisse

Mme Massé Paulette,
Villesavoir, Chouzy s/Cisse
41150 Onzain   tél. 54 79 38 06

Pers. suppl: 15F par jour
Jours suppl: 120F
Réservation: S.R.

AUBERGE DE JEUNESSE

59, Grand-Place – Ouvert toute l'année. 52 places, douches chaudes, repas aux groupes sur demande, possibilité de cuisiner. Située dans un ensemble architectural XVII-XVIIIe siècles très intéressant. Siège de l'Association départementale des A.J.

ONZAIN 41150 L.-et-Ch. 64 ⑥ – 3 021 h. alt. 67.
Paris 197 – Amboise 20 – Blois 16 – Château-Renault 24 – Montrichard 21 – ◆Tours 44.

⚜ **Domaine des Hauts de Loire** M ⑤, NO : 3 km par D 1 et voie privée ☎ 54
20 72 57, Télex 751547, ☎, « Manoir, parc et forêt », ✕ – ☑ ⚑ ᵃ ℗ – ᴁ 80.
ᴁ Ɛ ᴠ⍒ ⑤
15 *mars-1ᵉʳ déc.* – SC : R 195/300 – ☲ 52 – **22 ch** 836/970, 6 appartements
1 150/1 350
Spéc. Mousse de persil à l'huile de noisettes, Dos de sandre poêlé sauce au Bourgueil. Vins
Sauvignon, Touraine-Mesland.

🏠 **Château des Tertres** ⑤ *sans rest,* O : 1,5 km par D 58 ☎ 54 20 83 88, ⟨,
« Gentilhommière dans un parc » – 🛏wc 🛏wc ☎ ℗. ᴁ ᴠ⍒ ✕
22 *mars-2 nov.* – SC : ☲ 23 – **14 ch** 200/270.

PEUGEOT, TALBOT Gar. Guyader. ☎ 54 20 70   RENAULT Gar. Lemaire. ☎ 54 20 70 45
37 Ⓝ

Sais-tu dire où les gens voudraient être logés?

> **Monsieur Jones** voudrait un hôtel 5 étoiles.
> **M. et Mme Nutt** voudraient un hôtel 3 étoiles.
> **La famille Crump** voudrait un gîte.
> **Mlle Wilson et Mlle Tonks** voudraient l'Auberge de Jeunesse.
> **Mme Kelly** voudrait un Centre de Séjour.
> **Les équipes sportives** voudraient un camping.

Et maintenant à toi

M et Mme le maire
l'équipe de football
La famille Smith
L'orchestre
La famille Crump
Mells Wilson et Tonks
L'équipe de Rugby

Où vont-ils être logés?

You have a list of people in your party together with the accommodation each required. François only has the list of names and wants to know who wants what.

One of you takes the role of François and asks questions such as:

Que voudrait M. et Mme Smith?

Que voudrait l'orchestre?

The other has the list containing the information about accommodation and answers accordingly.

François then has to note down this information in order to make the necessary reservations.

Un peu de lecture

Les détails de l'hébergement

Some members of the party have asked for details about where they are going to stay.

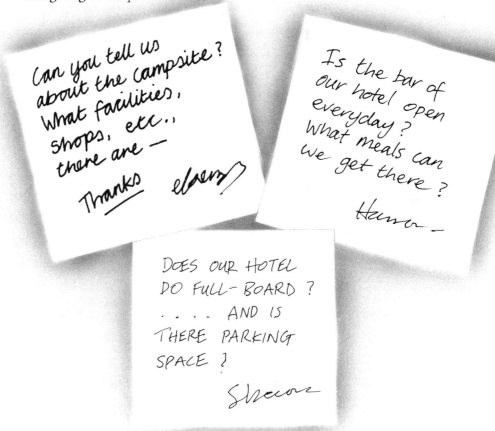

Can you tell us about the campsite? What facilities, shops, etc.. there are —

Thanks

Is the bar of our hotel open everyday? What meals can we get there?

DOES OUR HOTEL DO FULL-BOARD? . . . . AND IS THERE PARKING SPACE?

Can you write the answers to their notes? These are the places where they will stay:

Camping

La Guinguette **NN

EAU CHAUDE   *** ELECTRICITE

Entièrement rénovés les
**BAR - BRASSERIE - FRITERIE
ALIMENTATION GÉNÉRALE
Salle pour BANQUETS et RECEPTIONS**
Ouvert toute l'année

Sais-tu expliquer ce que certains doivent avoir comme hébergement – et pourquoi?

> Pour M. McDonald il faut une chambre au rez-de-chaussée.
> Il est handicappé.
>
> Pour l'équipe de football, il faut un camping isolé.
> Ils font beaucoup de bruit.
>
> Pour Mme Morgan il faut une chambre tranquille.
> Elle dort mal.

Et maintenant à toi

Les besoins particuliers

You have two lists of special requirements for your party of people, whereas François has only the names. Tell him who needs what in the first list. Your partner will take the role of François.

When you have completed this task, take the second list and reverse roles.

Mr et Mme Dunn
Mr Grimble
Melle Armour

Mme Atkinson
Mr et Mme Watson
La famille Allen.

Sais-tu dire ce qui n'est pas comme il faut?

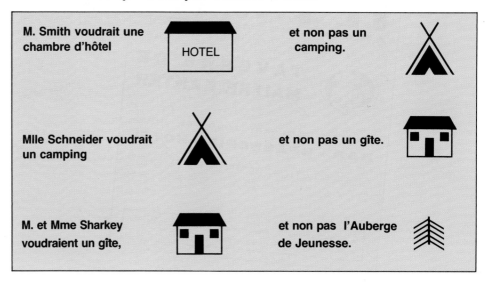

M. Smith voudrait une chambre d'hôtel — HOTEL — et non pas un camping.

Mlle Schneider voudrait un camping — et non pas un gîte.

M. et Mme Sharkey voudraient un gîte, — et non pas l'Auberge de Jeunesse.

Et maintenant à toi

On vérifie les réservations

Now check these accommodation requirements with François. Your partner will take the role of François, and will tell you what his booking arrangements are. Correct him if he's got it wrong.

Following the cards that your teacher will give you, your conversation should run like this:

> **e.g.** **François:** M. Smith voudrait un camping? C'est ça?
> **Toi:** Non, M. Smith voudrait le CISO, et non pas un camping.

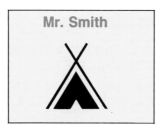

Mr. Smith

CISO

> or **François:** M. Sharkey voudrait un gîte? C'est ça?
> **Toi:** Oui, c'est ça! M. Sharkey voudrait un gîte.

Mr Sharkey

Un peu de lecture

Tout est comme il faut

Finally, check the complete list that François has left against yours here. If any mistakes have been made, make a note of required alterations to tell François.

M et Mme Nutt – hôtel
M Jones – CISO
Mme Kelly – hôtel
Orchestre – CISO
La famille Robinson – hôtel
M. McDonald – gîte
Melle Reed – Auberge de Jeunesse

Prends ton stylo

Un mot pour François

Can you write a note for François, telling him where he has gone wrong?

Un peu de lecture

Le transport

Your group has now settled in. To help you to respond to queries as quickly as possible, you have left a notepad in the reception area of the Town Hall for group members to leave messages when you are not available. One day you find a series of messages about transport. Leave answers to be picked up. You will need to study on the following pages the details about buses, taxis, etc., that François has given you.

PLEASE LEAVE ANY QUESTIONS OR QUERIES HERE IF I AM NOT IN.
I WILL DEAL WITH THEM AS SOON AS POSSIBLE.

Does the No. 1 bus run on Sundays?
How frequent is it on week-days? Mrs. Kelly.

Where does the Blois bus go from?
What time is the last bus back from Blois? M. Jones.

Does the taxi service operate day and night? Do you know how much the fare from the station to the stadium is likely to be?
P. McDonald.

Where does the Tours bus leave from in Tours and Onjain? How frequent is it? C. Reed.

TRANSPORTS EN COMMUN D'ONZAIN – GUIDE DU RESEAU

Ligne 1: Onzain – Chouzy

Departs: Onzain – Gare Routière.
Chouzy – Place du Vieux Marché.

circule de 5 h 40 à 21 h 15

FREQUENCE	HEURE POINTE MATIN	HEURE CREUSE MATIN	HEURE CREUSE APRES MIDI	HEURE POINTE APRES MIDI	NUIT
Semaine	22'	30'	30'	22'	50'
Samedi	30'	30'	30'	30'	50'
	MATINEE		APRES MIDI		NUIT
Dimanches et Fêtes	pas de service		de 30' à 55'		50'

Ligne 2: ONZAIN – BLOIS

Departs: Onzain – Gare Routière
Blois – Gare SNCF

circule de 6 h 00 à 22 h 00

FREQUENCE	HEURE POINTE MATIN	HEURE CREUSE MATIN	HEURE CREUSE APRES MIDI	HEURE POINTE APRES MIDI	NUIT
Semaine	15'	33'	22'	16'	40'
Samedi	25'	30'	24'	20'	40'
	MATINEE		APRES MIDI		NUIT
Dimanches et Fêtes	45'		30'		80'

Ligne 13: ONZAIN – TOURS

Departs: Onzain – Avenue de la République, Rive Droite.
Tours – Café du Musée.

circule de 5 h 30 à 21 h 00

FREQUENCE	HEURE POINTE MATIN	HEURE CREUSE MATIN	HEURE CREUSE APRES MIDI	HEURE POINTE APRES MIDI	NUIT
Semaine	10'	60'	35'	10'	NL.
Samedi				APRES MIDI	
	MATINEE				
Dimanches et Fêtes	1 départ			2 départs	

SERVICE ASSURE
24 h / 24
DIMANCHE
ET JOURS FERIES

ATTESTATION DE TRANSPORT

TAXI N° 33
LACOURTABLAISE J.M.
7, rue des Giroflées
66000 PERPIGNAN

0014548

Certifie avoir transporté M.

Demeurant

N° de sécurité sociale

de *Gare*

à *Stade*

Prix compteur

Jour, nuit, férié, dimanche

Autoroute

Bagages *avec*

SOMME A PAYER 29

PERPIGNAN, le 6/8/88   Signature du Conducteur

RECLAMATIONS adresser toute réclamation à l'Association des Taxis Radio, 8 bis, rue St Joseph, bureau où les chauffeurs déposent les objets trouvés dans leur voiture

TAXI ONZAIN

54.20.76.64

A VOTRE SERVICE
7 jours sur 7
*
TOUTES DISTANCES

Mme CHARPENTIER
2, RUE DE LA CROIX FOUGERE   41150 ONZAIN

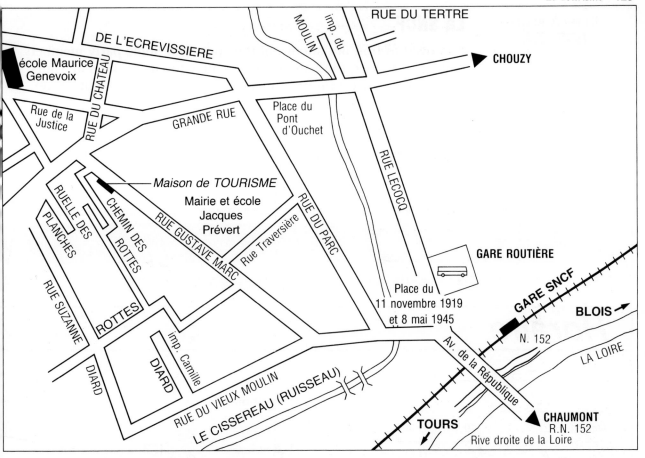

Sais-tu comprendre et poser des questions à propos des transports locaux?

A quelle heure part le bus pour ....?
Quand est-ce qu'il arrive à ....?
Où est l'arrêt des bus pour ....?
Combien ça coûte un billet?
                  un carnet?
Pour aller à ....?
Quel est le numéro de téléphone de ....?

Travaillez en groupe

SNCF
DEPART
➡

Les renseignements sur le transport

Appoint a 'courier' in the group. The others take the role of French visitors. Taking in turn the question cards which the teacher will provide, ask if the information shown is correct. The 'courier', using the Onzain information (opposite) will confirm that it is, or if it is not, will supply the correct information.

    e.g.   **Visitor:**   Le 13 part de la gare SNCF?
                  Courier: Non. Le 13 part de l'avenue de la République.

Un peu de lecture

La SNCF

You need to find out about rail transport too. Some party members may want to visit the famous Loire Valley towns of Blois or Tours, or indeed, may wish to travel to Paris, which is quite possible to do on a day trip.

Study this document which shows rail connections, times and prices between Onzain and Paris. Then write answers to the notes which have been left on the Town Hall reception notepad.

SNCF

Horaire

TOURS		06.40	11.00	16.20
AMBOISE		07.10	11.30	16.50
ONZAIN	A	07.21	11.51	17.11
	D	07.23	11.53	17.13
BLOIS		07.55	12.25	17.45
ORLEANS		09.03	13.20	18.40
PARIS		09.55	14.15	19.30
		🍴	⊗	✕

PARIS		09.20	13.10	18.30
ORLEANS		09.55	13.55	19.25
BLOIS		10.20	14.30	20.00
ONZAIN	A	10.48	15.00	20.28
	D	10.50	15.02	20.30
AMBOISE		11.06	15.18	20.48
TOURS		11.30	15.45	21.08
		🍴	✕	⊗

Symboles

A	Arrivée	🍽	Restauration à la place
D	Départ	🍷	Bar
⊨	Couchettes	🍴	Vente ambulante
🛏	Voiture-Lits	⬭	Trans Europ Express
✕	Voiture-restaurant	*IC*	Intercités
⊗	Grill-express	*TGV*	Train grande vitesse

SNCF

TARIFS A PARTIR D'ONZAIN	2e classe	
	Aller simple	Aller et retour
Tours	55F	110F
Amboise	35F	70F
Blois	40F	80F
Orléans	60F	120F
Paris	110F	220F
Enfants – demi-tarif		

PLEASE LEAVE ANY QUESTIONS OR QUERIES HERE IF I AM NOT IN.

I WILL DEAL WITH THEM AS SOON AS POSSIBLE

Can you let me know when the last train back from Paris gets in please? P McDonald.

Will it cost more than 200f for my wife + me to go to Tours for the day? Trump.

How much are the Adult and child return fares to Blois? thanks.

Is there a restaurant-service on all the Paris trains?   M. Jones.

Sais-tu parler des horaires?

> Le premier train pour Paris part à 06h00.
> Le prochain train pour Paris part à 9h00.
> Le dernier train part à 18h00.

Et maintenant à toi

A quelle heure part ...?

Practise these conversations with your partner. When you have both taken the two roles, make up some more. Make sure that the 'courier' has the railway timetables.

Courier	Visitor
A Je peux vous aider?	
	A quelle heure part le premier train pour Paris?
Il part à	
	Le voyage dure longtemps?
Il dure	
	Y a-t-il un buffet dans ce train?
Oui, il y a un buffet.	
	Merci beaucoup.
B Ask how you can help.	
	Ask if there is a train for Tours at about midday.
Say no but there is one at 15.00.	
	Ask for the departure time of the last train from Tours to Onzain.
Say what time this train leaves.	
	Ask what time the train arrives in Onzain.
Say what time this train arrives.	
	Thank the courier.

Un peu de lecture

Voiture à louer

Horace Jones, chairman of your town-twinning committee, wants to hire a medium-sized car. Study the documents about car-hire, and then try to write an answer to the note which he has sent you.

POUR LOUER UNE VOITURE

Être âgé de 21 ans pour conduire et contracter une location pour les catégories A-B-C, de 25 ans pour les catégories E-F-H-I-K-O-P-R-T-J et pour bénéficier d'une assurance complémentaire et de 30 ans pour la catégorie L.

Permis de conduire de plus d'un an.

Carte d'identité ou passeport.

Dans tous les cas il faut pouvoir justifier d'un domicile fixe et remplir les conditions fixées par la Fédération des Loueurs.

 **TARIF**

CATÉGORIES			MODÈLES	PORTES	RADIO	CAS.	JOUR		KM
ÉCONOMIQUE *SUBCOMPACT*		A	Renault 5 205 Junior	3 3	♪		HT TTC	160,00 **204,80**	2,00 **2,56**
		B	Peugeot 205 GL Renault Super 5 GL	5 5	♪		HT TTC	170,00 **217,60**	2,35 **3,01**
MOYENNE *MEDIUM SIZE*		C	Renault 11 Peugeot 309 Golf	4	♪		HT TTC	199,00 **254,72**	2,80 **3,58**
SUPÉRIEURE *FULL SIZE*		E	Renault 21 GTS Peugeot 405 GR	4 4	♪		HT TTC	258,00 **330,24**	3,50 **4,48**
		F	Renault 25 GTS	4 4	♪	⬚	HT TTC	294,00 **376,32**	3,70 **4,74**
AUTOMATIQUES	MOYENNE *MEDIUM*	H	Renault 11 TA Peugeot 205 TA	5 3	♪	⬚	HT TTC	217,00 **277,76**	2,40 **3,07**
	SUPÉRIEURE *FULL SIZE*	I	Renault 25 TA	4	♪	⬚	HT TTC	311,00 **398,08**	3,30 **4,22**
	LUXE *LUXURY*	K*	Mercedes 190 E Renault 25 GTX	4 4	♪	⬚	HT TTC	371,00 **474,88**	3,70 **4,74**
		L*	Mercedes 230 E	4	♪	⬚	HT TTC	474,00 **606,72**	5,20 **6,66**

TO: The English Courier

From: Horace Jones

Can you get me some info on car-hire Please?
I would like a medium-sized car for a few days,
and would like to know:

    (i) which cars are available;

    (ii) the cost per day (with and without tax);

    (iii) the cost per kilometre;

    (iv) the minimum hire period;

    (v) the cost of insurance;

    (vi) what papers I need to produce.

I'd appreciate your help.

      Thanks a lot

        Horace Jones.

Ecoute la cassette (2)

FIDO

Coinciding with the town-twinning events is the Foire Internationale D'Onzain (FIDO), a trade fair, and more entertainment and sport than usual.

François tells you where the principal side-events will take place. Can you mark them on your map as he tells you?

Sais-tu parler des attractions?

Il y a le stade	**pour jouer au football.**
Il y a le parc d'attractions	**c'est une foire.**
Il y a la piscine	**pour nager.**
Il y a le château	**qui date du 15e siècle.**
Il y a le théâtre	**pour aller voir des pièces.**
Il y a le théâtre antique	**qui date de l'époque des Romains.**
Il y a le cinéma	**pour aller voir les films.**
Il y a la pâtinoire	**pour pâtiner.**
Il y a la salle des fêtes	**pour jouer au ping-pong, etc.**
Il y a la discothèque	**pour écouter la musique, et pour danser.**

Un peu de lecture

FIDOSCOPE

François has given you some information about events organised during FIDO week. What would you choose?

Le Quartier Latin
Discothèque

Soirée   Défilé

Spectacle   Séminaire

Toutes les Soirées sauf dimanche.
20.00 – 03.00   Entrée: 40f.00.

PISCINE D'ONZAIN

Grand Concours International
Mercredi de 14.00 a 18.00

•

Piscine disponible aux visiteurs toutes matinées de 07.00 a 12.00.

SOIRÉE DE GALA
avec ORCHESTRE DANSANT
À
Route de la Vallée des Rois

CHAUMONT

VAL DE LOIRE/FRANCE

Téléphone: Onzain 54.20.98.03 (château) – 54.20.93.99 (écuries)

Ouvert tous les jours, sauf les 1ᵉʳ janvier, 1ᵉʳ mai, 1ᵉʳ et 11 novembre, 25 décembre

Dimanche le 22 à 18.00: Réservations nécessaires

LES P'TITS SCHTROUMPFS
de Peyo
LE FILM

UN GRAND DESSIN ANIMÉ

CINÉMA UTOPIE

ENTRÉE:

ADULTES: 25 f.00.
ENFANTS: 10 f.00.

FREQUENCE MEURTRE
Tlj.: 13 h 40 – 15 h 50 – 18 h – 20 h 10 – 22 h 15   POLICIER

L'INSOUTENABLE LEGERETE DE L'ETRE
(V.O.-son Dolby Stéréo)
Tlj.: 13 h 50 – 17 h 20 – 20 h 50   PSYCHOLOGIQUE

CRY FREEDOM (le Cri de la Liberté)
(V.O.-son Dolby Stéréo)
Tlj.: 14 h – 17 h 30 – 21 h   POLITIQUE

EMPIRE DU SOLEIL
(V.O.-son Dolby Stéréo)
Tlj. (sauf je.) 13 h 50 – 17 h 20 – 20 h 50 –
je.: 17 h 20 – 20 h 50   HISTOIRE

SEPTEMBER
Tlj.: 14h (V.F.) – 16h (V.F.) – 18h (V.O.) – 20h
(V.O.) – 22h (V.O.)   ROMANTIQUE

Sais-tu comprendre des questions sur les attractions?

> **A quelle heure commence le match de rugby?**
> **A combien sont les places pour le cinéma?**
> **Faut-il réserver pour la soirée de gala?**
> **Y-a-t-il un tarif spécial pour les groupes?**

. . . . et donner les réponses?

> **Le match du rugby? Il commence à 10h00.**
> **Le cinéma? Les places sont à 25f.00**
> **La soirée de gala? Oui, il faut réserver.**
> **Non, il n'y a pas de tarif spécial.**

Ecoute la cassette (3)

FIDOSPORTS

You take a phone call from the manager of the **Stade d'Onzain**, telling you what sporting and other events have been arranged at the Stade during FIDO. Make a grid like the one here and note them down.

	HEURE	ATTRACTION	LIEU
Lundi			
Mardi			
Mercredi			
Jeudi			
Vendredi			
Samedi			
Dimanche			

Un peu de lecture

Une journée à Paris

François has arranged a coach-trip to Paris for the day for the English group. Here is the proposed itinerary:

Hotel de Ville d'Onzain

Onzain, le ___14 septembre___

Excursion à Paris - Itinéraire

06.00   Départ Onzain, Hôtel de Ville.

08.00   Pause-pipi vers Orléans.

10.00   Arrive Paris, Place Charles de Gaulle-Etoile.

10.00 à 13.00 Tour Guidé de Paris en car, y compris:
Arc de Triomphe, Place de la Concorde, Invalides, Louvre, Notre Dame, Quartier Latin, Basilique du Sacré-Coeur.

13.00 à 15.00 Arrêt à Montmartre.
(Vous pouvez visiter la Place du Tertre, quartier des artistes, où vous trouverez plusieurs petits restaurants, pour prendre le repas de midi.)

15.00   Départ Montmartre.

15.30 à 18.30 Arrêt Place de l'Opéra.
(Shopping, Galeries Lafayette, rue de Rivoli, etc.)

19.00   Départ Paris.

23.00   Arrive Onzain.

Rue Gustave Marc, 41150 ONZAIN   Tél: 54 00 11 00

François asks you to get to know this programme, as there are bound to be many questions about it. In fact, a number of notes have been left in the office. Can you sort out the answers to the queries?

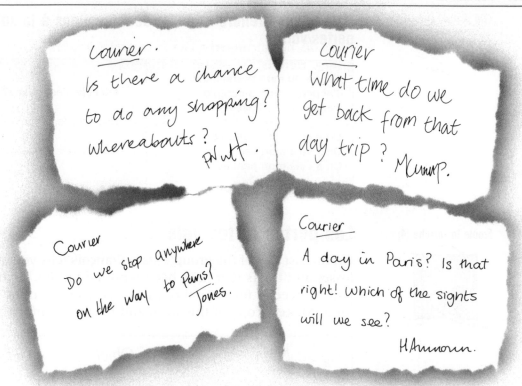

Courier.
Is there a chance to do any shopping? Whereabouts?
Pratt.

Courier
What time do we get back from that day trip?
McKinup.

Courier
Do we stop anywhere on the way to Paris?
Jones.

Courier
A day in Paris? Is that right! Which of the sights will we see?
H. Amnonn.

Sais-tu parler de ce qu'on va faire?

> On va quitter Onzain à 6h00.
> On va arriver à Paris à 10h00.
> On va visiter la tour Eiffel.
> On va déjeuner à Montmartre.

Et maintenant à toi

Une excursion

Divide the cards which the teacher will give you into two piles, turned face downwards. Take turns to expose them and to announce what they show. They are all parts of a day-trip itinerary.

e.g. On va quitter Onzain à 08h00.

When all the cards are exposed, put them in order. They could then be used as part of a poster for the day-trip.

Sais-tu comprendre et poser des questions à la suite des pertes/vols?

J'ai perdu mon portefeuille. J'ai perdu mon parapluie. J'ai perdu mon passeport. On a volé mon portemonnaie. On a volé mon sac à main. On a volé mon pantalon.	Où cela s'est passé? Décrivez-le, s'il vous plaît. Combien il vaut, votre ....?

Ecoute la cassette (4)

Les pertes et les vols

On the last day of the group's stay, François tells you about a number of losses and thefts that have been reported to him. As this information will be needed for insurance purposes, you fill in the official report form. Make a copy of this form and fill in the information required.

Nom	Objet	Perdu ou volé
1. Horace Jones	Portefeuille brun	Perdu
2.		
3.		
4.		

J'ai perdu mon portefeuille!

Et maintenant à toi

Des problèmes!

Travaille avec ton collègue.

You need to report to François the items which have been lost or stolen during your group's stay. He asks you some questions which you answer, using the cards provided.

François	Courier
De qui s'agit-il? Et de quoi s'agit-il? Où cela s'est passé? Combien il/elle vaut . . . ? Décrivez-le/la, s'il vous plaît.	Horace Jones Portefeuille à l'hôtel 200 à 500fs brun

When you have worked through the cards, change roles, and then make up some more conversations like this.

Vocabulaire

accompagnateur (*m*)   group leader or organiser

accompagner   to accompany

aider   to help

aller (et) retour (*m*)   return ticket

aller simple (*m*)   single ticket

arrêt (*m*)   stop (bus stop, etc)

arrêter   to stop

attestation (*f*)   evidence/certificate

auberge (*f*)   inn

auberge de jeunesse (*f*)   youth-hostel

besoin (*m*)   need

bruit (*m*)   noise

camping (*m*)   camping

centre de séjour (*m*)   hostel

château (*m*)   castle

cinéma (*m*)   cinema

coûter   to cost

demi-tarif (*m*)   half price

dernier(e)   next

discothèque (*f*)   disco

disponible   available

distractions (*f*)   entertainment

durer   to last

dégustation (*f*)   tasting/sampling

électricité (*f*)   electricity

équipe (*f*)   team

friterie (*f*)   chip shop

fruits de mer (*m*)   sea food

gîte rural (*m*)   self-catering holiday home

hébergement (*m*)   accommodation

hôtel (*m*)   hotel

isolé   isolated/lonely

journée (*f*)   day/day out

loger   to lodge, provide accommodation

orchestre (*m*)   orchestra/band

ouvert(e)   open

parapluie (*m*)   umbrella

parc d'attractions (*m*)   fun-fair

partir   to leave

passeport (*m*)   passport

patinoire (*m*)   skating-rink

portefeuille (*m*)   wallet

portemonnaie (*m*)   purse

problème (*m*)   problem

prochain(e)   next

réseau (*m*)   network

sac à main (*m*)   handbag

salle des fêtes (*f*)   village hall

stade (*m*)   stadium

tarif (*m*)   price

théâtre (*m*)   theatre

théâtre antique (*m*)   Roman theatre (ruins)

tranquille   peaceful

transport en commun (*m*)   public transport

vérifier   to check

UNITÉ

La Maison de Tourisme

Following your success in acting as courier for your town-twinning exchange, you are offered the chance to work in the Tourist Office in Onzain during July and August. Your employers are delighted to allow you to take up the offer.

At the end of this unit you should be able to:

1 Understand and tell people about the weather.
2 Give directions to places as required.
3 Give information about places of interest.
4 Make **gîte** and restaurant reservations.

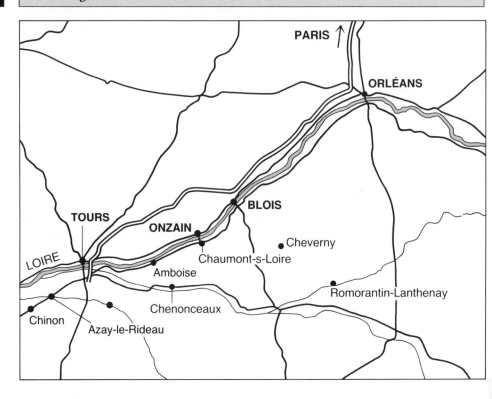

Ecoute la cassette (1)

Quel temps fait-il?

As you work in the Tourist Office, people often ask you about the weather. Note down what each person wants to know.

MAISON DE TOURISME D'ONZAIN
Rue Gustave Marc, Onzain 41150
Tél: 54 22 12 22

Sais-tu dire quel temps il fait?/va faire?

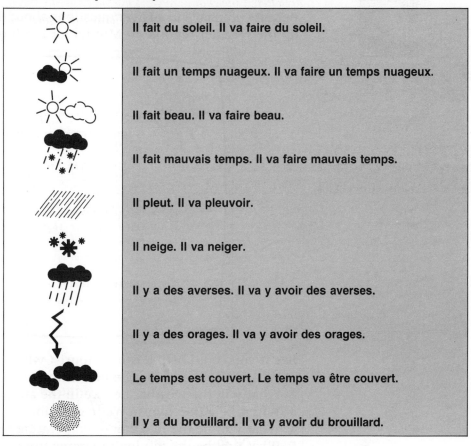

Il fait du soleil. Il va faire du soleil.

Il fait un temps nuageux. Il va faire un temps nuageux.

Il fait beau. Il va faire beau.

Il fait mauvais temps. Il va faire mauvais temps.

Il pleut. Il va pleuvoir.

Il neige. Il va neiger.

Il y a des averses. Il va y avoir des averses.

Il y a des orages. Il va y avoir des orages.

Le temps est couvert. Le temps va être couvert.

Il y a du brouillard. Il va y avoir du brouillard.

Et maintenant à toi

La météo

Travaille avec ton collègue.

Listen again to the three speakers and, using the information below, try to work out together what answer you would give and then practise the dialogue.

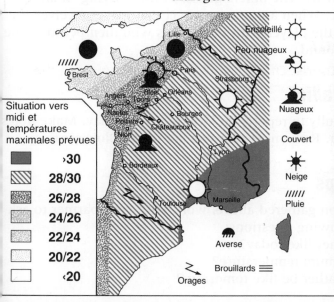

Situation vers midi et températures maximales prévues

▨	›30
▨	28/30
▨	26/28
▨	24/26
▨	22/24
▨	20/22
☐	‹20

Ensoleillé
Peu nuageux
Nuageux
Couvert
Neige
Pluie
Averse
Orages
Brouillards ≡

Aujourd'hui dans la région : : temps lourd avec orages parfois forts l'après-midi. Vent variable faible s'orientant au secteur sud modéré. Violentes rafales sous orages.

Températures prévues aujourd'hui (mini/max)

Angers	16/28	Châteauroux	16/28	Poitiers	14/29
Blois	15/28	Niort	16/28	Tours	15/28
Bourges	15/29	Orléans	14/28		

Les marées aujourd'hui:

Coef.		Pte de Grave	La Rochelle	St-Nazaire
57	hautes	4.59 – 17.10	4.41 – 16.56	4.31 – 16.50
61	basses	10.39 – 23.06	10.18 – 22.52	10.49 – 23.12

Extrait de l'annuaire des marées du S.H.O.M. et reproduit avec son autorisation

Mercredi 10 août: lever du soleil : 6 h 38; coucher : 21 h 13.

Fêtes à souhaiter : sainte Claire, sainte Gilberte, sainte Suzanne (Suzel, Suzette, Suzon, Suzy).

Un peu de lecture

La météo sur Minitel

Because you have to answer questions about the weather you often look up the weather reports on Minitel for the Blois area.

MÉTÉO SUR MINITEL
RÉGION DE BLOIS

```
 9h00  Il va faire un temps nuageux.
12h00  Il va faire beau sur toute la région.
18h00  Il va faire encore beau mais avec des orages.
00h00  Il va y avoir des orages.

       Températures maximales - 26°
       Températures minimales - 14°
```

See if you could help a British tourist who asked these questions:
1 What will the weather be like in the morning?
2 What will the weather be like in the afternoon?
3 Will it be a fine night? We're camping!
4 What will be the maximum temperature?
5 What will be the minimum temperature?

Travaillez en groupe

Le jeu du temps

Play this game together. The group leader holds the cards with the weather symbols, hidden so that the others cannot see them. S/he then asks 'Quel temps fait-il?' The others guess, in turn, saying 'Il fait du soleil?' 'Il pleut?' etc. When a guess is correct that player receives the card. The winner is the player with most cards who then becomes the leader for the next round.

Ecoute la cassette (2)

La météo à la radio

You also listen carefully to reports on local radio each day. Make notes about what you hear. Remember that you are in the Blois area.

Et maintenant à toi

Parlons du temps

Using the information gathered above, work with your partner to ask and answer the following questions:
1 What is the weather like today?
2 What is the maximum temperature?
3 What will the weather be like tomorrow?

Un peu de lecture

Le mot d'une collègue

One day you find this note on your desk from a colleague in the Town Hall. What does she want?

Hotel de Ville d'Onzain

Rue Gustave Marc, ONZAIN 41150   Tél: 54 00 11 00

Onzain, le _____

Je pars ce soir en Angleterre. Quel temps fait-il à Londres ?

Prends ton stylo

Le temps à Londres

Using the information in the weather report below, write one or two sentences in French in answer to the note.

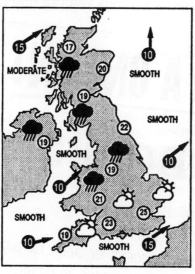

Afternoon

MODERATE
SMOOTH
SMOOTH
SMOOTH
SMOOTH
SMOOTH

15 17 10 20 19 22 10 19 19 10 21 10 23 25 19 15

General outlook
....

Southern areas will stay dry with the best of the sunshine.

London, SE England, Central S England, Channel Is, SW England. Dry. Broken cloud and intervals of sunshine. Max 25C (77f).

Ecoute la cassette (3)

Des personnes vous demandent où il faut aller

Five people come into the Tourist Office one morning all wanting to find a different service in Onzain. Jot down what they want.

Un peu de lecture

Il faut aller là

Using the advertisements below and the notes you have made, decide where you will recommend each person to go.

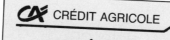

GARAGE GUYADER
Location tous véhicules
Ventes et dépannages rapides
toutes marques
1, av. de la République
ONZAIN   TÉL. 54.20.70.37

CA CRÉDIT AGRICOLE
Quelle que soit votre activité
une solution à vos problèmes

CRÉDIT AGRICOLE MUTUEL

HERBAULT – Tél. 54.46.13.24
Sur la Grande-Place 11, rue de la Justice
ONZAIN – Tél. 54.20.71.20

ANNICK
Coiffure Hommes et Dames
Parfumerie – Soins esthétiques
Tél. 54.20.72.12 *sur rendez-vous*
6, rue du Pont d'Ouchet –
ONZAIN

optique baron
D.E.S.O.
Tl. 54.20.75.78
ARNOPTIC s.a.r.l.
4, Grande-Rue   41150 ONZAIN

Pour tous vos achats.
Choix et qualité
Brodequins – Bottes
Chaussures de ville et de sport
Chaussures GARANNE
ONZAIN   18, Grande-Rue
Tel. 54.20.74.58

Un peu de lecture

On achète des cadeaux

Tourists often ask you where they can buy gifts in Onzain. A new shop is opening shortly so you decide to recommend it.
1 When is it opening?
2 Write a list of 4 things you can buy there.

NOUVEAU A ONZAIN !

FRAMBOISINE

— *des idées pour tous* —

CADEAUX,
VANNERIE,
DECOR DE LA MAISON,
GADGETS,

BIBELOTS,
ROTIN,
JOUETS ET JEUX EN BOIS,
PORCELAINE BLANCHE,

FLEURS SECHEES,
PELUCHES,
ETC...

OUVERTURE DÉBUT AOUT

22, GRAND'RUE 41150 ONZAIN TEL : 54 20 79 19

Le château de Chaumont

The nearest castle to Onzain is Chaumont-sur-Loire. You can see it across the river. Jot down the revised details about its opening times for a British tourist.

CHAUMONT-SUR-LOIRE

La tour de l'Ouest, l'aile sud, l'entrée et l'aile est. Phot. J. Feuillie, Cnmhs.

Depuis la rive droite de la Loire. Phot. A. Lonchampt - Cnmhs. ▷

LE CHATEAU

Du 1er avril au 30 septembre
9h. - 11h20
13h30 - 17h20

41150 Chaumont-sur-Loire / Onzain
Tél. : (16) 54.20.98.03
Monument historique d'Etat / Ministère de la Culture
Direction du Patrimoine.

Pour en savoir plus sur ce monument :
Melot (Michel) et Melet-Sanson (Jacqueline) : *le château de Chaumont.*
Ed. Cnmhs.

Caisse Nationale des Monuments Historiques et des Sites.
Ministère de la Culture.

Hôtel Sully. 62, rue Saint-Antoine
75004 Paris. Tél. : 274.22.22.

© CNMHS - 1985 - Texte: C. Legros - Maquette: Crespel-BdC - Imprimerie Blanchard 01.1987

Le passeport des loisirs

The **passeport des loisirs** is given to tourists so that they can get reductions on the price of entry to certain castles and museums.

The person who worked in the tourist office before you has left you this list of selective reductions. Use it to answer some questions from British tourists.

MAISON DE TOURISME D'ONZAIN

Rue Gustave Marc, Onzain 41150
Tél: 54 22 12 22

Visite	Tarif Normal	Tarif Etudiant	Prix Passeport des Loisirs
Château de Chambord	25^{F}50	21^{F}30	18^F
Château de Blois	28^F	24^F	20^{F}5
Château d'Amboise	30^F	27^{F}50	25^F
Musée de Sologne à Romorantin	15^F	13^{F}80	12^F+5 (sauf dimanche jours de fê...
Sinfonietta de Chambord	15^F	12^{F}50	10^F
Cinéma Palace à Blois	25^F	22^{F}50	20^F (le dimanch...

1 How much less will we have to pay at Chambord?
2 Can we get a reduction at Amboise? If so how much?
3 Will it be cheaper at the museum in Romorantin and can we go on Sundays?
4 Can we get a reduction every evening at the Cinema Palace in Blois?

Sais-tu parler des prix?

C'est combien l'entrée du château?
C'est combien avec réduction?
C'est vingt-cinq francs.
C'est treize francs avec réduction.
C'est dix francs pour les adultes et cinq francs pour les enfants.
C'est gratuit pour les enfants.
Il y une réduction . . . pour les jeunes . . . pour les étudiants . . . pour les personnes âgées?

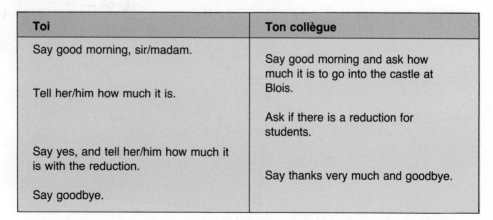

Et maintenant à toi

Tarifs réduits

Travaille avec ton collègue.

Using the information about reductions, ask and answer the following questions:

Toi	Ton collègue
Say good morning, sir/madam.	Say good morning and ask how much it is to go into the castle at Blois.
Tell her/him how much it is.	Ask if there is a reduction for students.
Say yes, and tell her/him how much it is with the reduction.	Say thanks very much and goodbye.
Say goodbye.	

Now work out a conversation for other places on the list opposite.

Le tourisme en famille

A family with children of different ages comes into the Tourist Office. They are looking for activities to interest them all. You sort out some brochures.

What can you offer:
1 the older boy and girl (15 and 16)
2 the younger boys (5 and 8)
3 the parents who are interested in crafts?

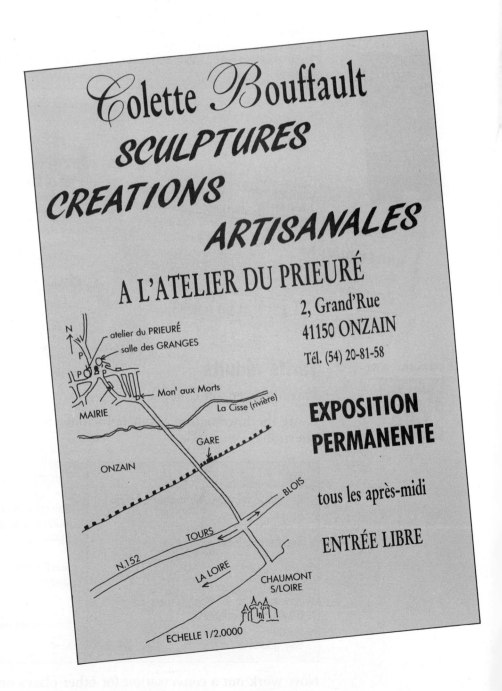

une journée
de rêve en
CANÖE

2 Parcours:

De Mennetou/cher
à Chabris
OU

De St Aignan
à Montrichard

la descente
du cher

C´EST SUPER !

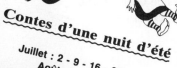

FOUGÈRES-SUR-BIÈVRE (41)
SON ET LUMIÈRE

Contes d'une nuit d'été

Juillet : 2 - 9 - 16 - 23 - 30
Août : 6 - 12 - 13

Un peu de lecture

Circuit en hélicoptère

Sometimes your clients want something quite unusual. A group of five tourists come looking for a tour of the castles with a difference. You suggest one of the trips below. Make a note of the details of each of the proposed trips. Use a grid like the one below:

Circuit no.	Prix	Durée
1		
2		
3		
4		
5		

5 CIRCUITS AU DEPART DE BLOIS-HELISTATION

Pont Charles de Gaulle, sortie Blois-Vienne, D.951

EN JUILLET ET AOUT
Réservation Héliport de 10 h à 13 h et de 14 h à 19 h

● CIRCUIT 1
Un vol baptême de l'air à 110 F par personne durée 5 minutes

● CIRCUIT 2
Un vol 220 F par personne, durée 10 minutes: Ménars / Chambord.

● CIRCUIT 3
Un circuit 375 F par personne, durée 17 minutes: Ménars / Chambord / Villesavin / Cheverny / Beauregard.

● CIRCUIT 4
Un circuit à 650 F par personne, durée 30 minutes, 100 km survolant: St-Denis / Ménars / Chambord / Villesavin / La Sistière / Cheverny / Troussay / Fougères / Chaumont / Beauregard.

● CIRCUIT 5
Un circuit à 1300 F par personne, durée 1 heure, 200 km survolant: St-Denis / Ménars / Chambord / Villesavin / La Sistière / Cheverny / Troussay / Fougères / Chenonceaux / Vallée de la Loire / Amboise.

Where should they book for all the trips?

Between what times is this booking-office open?

Un peu de lecture

Croisières sur la Loire

There are boat trips available on the river Loire. Read the information here and note down these details so that you can help tourists:

1 where it leaves from
2 times of departure
3 which days there are trips
4 how long each trip lasts
5 how much it costs
6 where you have to buy the tickets.

CROISIÈRES SUR LA LOIRE
A BORD DU LÉONARD DE VINCI

● Au départ de CHAUMONT à 15 h et à 17 h
Tous les dimanches jusqu'au 30 OCTOBRE
Tous les jours du 1ᵉʳ JUILLET au 15 SEPTEMBRE
Durée 1 h 30 aller-retour. Prix : 45 F, enfants : 25 F
Commentaire sur l'histoire de la marine de Loire
BILLETTERIE SUR LE BATEAU

COMPAGNIE DE NAVIGATION DE LA LOIRE
41150 ONZAIN

Sais-tu parler des visites ou des sorties?

> D'où part le bateau/l'autobus?

> Il part de Blois.

> A quelle heure?

> Il part à 8 heures.

> Combien de temps dure le voyage?

> Il dure une heure et demie.

> Non, c'est le jeudi et le samedi.

> C'est tous les jours?

> Oui, c'est tous les jours.

> Où achète-t-on les billets?

> On achète les billets sur l'autobus.

> C'est combien?

> C'est 45f pour les adultes et 30f pour les enfants.

Et maintenant à toi

Une sortie en bâteau

1 A French family with two adults and two children want to go on a boat trip. Work out the following role-play with your partner.

Toi	Ton collègue
Say good morning, sir/madam.	
	Say good morning and you would like to go on the river Loire.
Say there are trips from Chaumont every day.	

2 Using the information on the previous page, try to continue the role-play.

Toi	Ton collègue
Ask how much it is for adults and for children.	Give the answer.
Ask if there is a commentary and how long the trip lasts.	Give the answer.
Ask where you can buy the tickets.	Tell him/her.
Say thank you and goodbye.	Say goodbye.

Ecoute la cassette (4)

Excursion en car

A French tourist wants some information about two coach trips which are offered. Listen carefully and make a note of the four questions he asks.

Un peu de lecture

Informer un touriste

Look at the information opposite and see if you can work out what you would tell the tourist who wants to know about the two coach trips.

VOTRE AUTOCAR

LES CIRCUITS DES CHATEAUX

TARIF	
Prix (droits d'entrée compris) *Price (admittance included)*	90,00 F
Étudiants - Cartes Vermeil *Students*	75,00 F
Enfants 5-10 ans *Children 5-10 years*	50,00 F

RENSEIGNEMENTS et POINTS DE VENTE

2, place Victor-Hugo - BLOIS

Tél. 54 78 15 66

OFFICE DE TOURISME
Pavillon Anne-de-Bretagne
ou auprès du conducteur

N° 1 - Circuit François Ier
AMBOISE - CHENONCEAU
Mardi, jeudi, samedi
Tuesday, Thursday, Saturday

N° 2 - Circuit Grande Vénerie
CHAMBORD - CHEVERNY
Dimanche, lundi, mercredi, vendredi
Sunday, Monday, Wednesday, Friday

Renault Conseil, Tours

Et maintenant à toi

Les circuits des châteaux

Your partner will play the part of the French tourist. See if you can answer the questions.

Ton collègue	Toi
C'est combien, le circuit, s'il vous plaît? C'est combien pour un étudiant? C'est quels jours le circuit de Chambord et Cheverny? Je peux acheter le billet dans le car?	

Changez de rôles.

Et maintenant à toi

Les horaires des cars

Using the information below, ask and answer questions about the times the coach leaves and arrives at places on the tour.

Toi	Ton collègue
A quelle heure le car quitte-t-il la gare de Blois?	A treize heures quarante-cinq (à deux heures moins le quart).
A quelle heure le car arrive-t-il à Amboise?	A seize heures trente (à quatre heures et demie).

AMBOISE - CHENONCEAU

BLOIS – S.N.C.F.	13 h 45
BLOIS – Place Victor-Hugo	13 h 50
CHENONCEAU	14 h 30
AMBOISE	16 h 30
BLOIS – S.N.C.F.	18 h 40
BLOIS – Auberge de Jeunesse	18 h 50

CHAMBORD – CHEVERNY

BLOIS – S.N.C.F.	13 h 45
BLOIS – Place Victor-Hugo	13 h 50
CHAMBORD	14 h 15
CHEVERNY	16 h 30
BLOIS – S.N.C.F.	18 h 40
BLOIS – Auberge de Jeunesse	18 h 50

Un peu de lecture

Les touristes hollandais

You have some information about castles which are visited on a coach trip. Some Dutch tourists are planning a trip and you write a few notes for them in English. Write one or two facts about each of the castles.

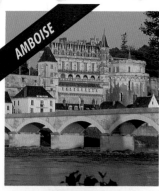
AMBOISE

Construit au XVI siècle. Emplacement d'une forteresse médiévale. Jolies salles meublées. Belle chapelle.

CHENONCEAU

Construit au XVI siècle. Diane de Poitiers y habitait. Joli pont sur le Cher. Emplacement d'un vieux moulin.

CHEVERNY

Construit au VII siècle. Décor de l'époque de Louis XIII. A visiter – musée de la Chasse. Toujours habité.

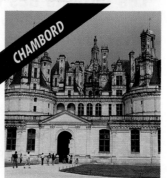
CHAMBORD

Construit au XVI siècle. Très grand château. Entouré de forêts. Grand escalier en pierre à double révolution.

Sais-tu comprendre les guides touristiques?

horaires d'ouverture	habité
fermé	décoré
visite guidée	meublé
un château	en dehors de la saison
une abbaye	un renseignement
aire (de pique-nique) (de jeux)	une propriété
privé	construit
renaissance	

Sais-tu faire le guide?

bâtir	le passé
un emplacement	assassiner
une forteresse	un monument
un spectacle	une résidence
un siècle	construit
seizième siècle	un escalier

Sais-tu comprendre et dire l'année?

1992 – mil neuf cent quatre-vingt-douze
1432 – mil quatre cent trente-deux
1974 – mil neuf cent soixante-quatorze
1556 – mil cinq cent cinquante-six

Travaillez en groupe

Le jeu de l'an 2000

On the table lay out two sets of cards face downwards. Taking it in turns, each player draws from set A and says, for example, 'Monsieur Boulanger a 25 ans. Il est né en 1975.' (This is the year 2000, remember). S/he then turns over a card from set B. If it says 1975 s/he keeps the card. The winner is the person with most paired cards.

Sais-tu parler des rois de France?

Louis XIV – quatorze   (1638–1715)
Henri III – trois   (1551–1589)
François I – premier   (1494–1547)
Louis XII – douze   (1462–1515)
Charles V – cinq   (1337–1380)

Un peu de lecture

Le 'cavern' du père Roland

Some English tourists are going to visit Amboise and ask you where
they should eat. You have heard good reports of the 'Cavern du Père
Roland.'

They will want to know: what kind of food it is – will there be much
choice – is it expensive – is it open on Tuesdays – can they park their
car nearby?

Et maintenant à toi

Réservation de table

The English tourists ask you to phone and book a table for five on
Tuesday evening about 7.30 p.m. They want to know if there is a special
menu for children. It will be four adults and a child.

Phone the restaurant. Your partner will play the part of the 'patron'.

Sais-tu louer une chambre ou un gîte?

un logement la location meublé l'accueil la pension complète	Je voudrais réserver un gîte. Pour quelles dates? C'est de la part de qui? Voulez-vous confirmer par écrit?

Un peu de lecture

Les gîtes

People often ask you for information about gîtes. Read the information about the different types. What services are offered?

Le gîte rural est une maison meublée à la campagne.

Le gîte d'étape accueille les gens qui ne veulent passer qu'une nuit et qui continuent leur route le lendemain.

Les chambres d'hôte sont des chambres dans des maisons et qui offrent la nuitée – c'est-à-dire le coucher et le petit déjeuner.

La table d'hôte – c'est quand les vacanciers en camping ou en chambre d'hôte peuvent manger chez le propriétaire.

Ce sont de petits terrains de camping situés sur des fermes. La limite est de 6 emplacements.

Le gîte d'enfants se spécialise dans l'accueil des enfants de 6 à 13 ans seuls sans leurs parents.

Chartres
A 200 kms de Paris

LE PERCHE

Loir

VENDÔME

LE LOIR VENDÔMOIS

A10

Loire

BLOIS

LA VALLÉE DE LA LOIRE

LA SOLOGNE

Tours

LA VALLÉE DU CHER

Cher

ROMORANTIN

Vierzon Bourges

Quel service faut-il?

Some tourists ask you for accommodation. Decide which type is best for each one. Link the numbers with the lettered symbols.

a   b   c

d   e   f

Et maintenant à toi

Les gîtes expliqués

Using the information you have learned, explain to your partner what each service is.

e.g. Ton collègue: Qu'est-ce que c'est qu'un gîte d'enfants?

Toi: Le gîte enfants spécialise dans l'accueil des enfants de 6 à 13 ans.

Demande d'hébergement

One day you get a phone call asking for accommodation. Copy this form into your book and note down, under the headings, what is wanted.

MAISON DE TOURISME D'ONZAIN
Rue Gustave Marc, Onzain 41150
Tél: 54 22 12 22

Nom du demandeur	Hébergement demandé	Dates	Enfants	Animaux	Autres demandes

Un peu de lecture

Les gîtes ruraux

You have the following information about some holiday homes which may be available. Which one do you think would be suitable for Mme Lenoir?

LES GITES RURAUX

Les gîtes que nous vous proposons sont des gîtes 3 épis. Ils ont été créés dans des anciens bâtiments de ferme où ils forment encore un ensemble avec les divers bâtiments d'exploitation et notre maison d'habitation.

GITE N° 138:
Rez-de-chaussée, séjour-cuisine, cheminée, prise T.V.,
Salle de bain
Trois chambres
Chauffage électrique, machine à laver, location de T.V., terrasse, animaux non admis.

GITE N° 189:
Rez de chaussée, séjour-cuisine, prise T.V.,
Salle de bain
Deux chambres
Chauffage central, machine à laver, location de T.V., terrasse, animaux admis.

GITE N° 27:
A l'étage, séjour-cuisine, prise T.V.,
Salle de bain
Deux chambres
Chauffage central, machine à laver, location de T.V., terrasse, animaux admis.

Ecoute la cassette (7)

Gîtes disponibles

Several tourists have approached you about renting gîtes for the weekend. Listen carefully to the announcements on local radio, which give the most recent information on gîtes available in the area. Compare it with the official list for the week (below) and sort out which gîtes are still available.

Note down in French any new gîtes which have become available.

Gîtes disponibles: Semaine du 5 août

Gîte No. 243
A l'étage, séjour, cuisine-salle à manger, T.V. couleur, salle de bain, une chambre, chauffage central.

Gîte No. 302
Rez de chaussée, séjour, coin cheminé, prise T.V., cuisine, deux chambres, salle de bain, chauffage central, terrasse.

Gîte No. 34
Rez de chaussée, séjour-cuisine, trois chambres, salle d'eau, chauffage électrique, machine à laver.

Vocabulaire

abbaye (f)	abbey	**marine** (f)	navy/boat traffic
accueil (m)	welcome/reception	**mauvais**	nasty, bad
aire de pique-nique (f)	picnic area	**meublé**	furnished
assassiner	to assassinate/kill	**moulin** (m)	mill
averse (f)	shower of rain	**musée** (m)	museum
bâtir	to build	**neiger**	to snow
beau, belle	fine, beautiful	**nuageux**	cloudy
brouillard (m)	fog	**nuitée** (f)	overnight stay
cadeau (m)	present, gift	**orage** (m)	storm
campagne (f)	countryside	**ouvert**	open
château (m)	castle	**ouverture** (f)	opening
circuit (m)	circuit/tour	**passé** (m)	past
coiffure (f)	hairstyle	**peluche** (f)	plush, soft toys
construit	built	**pierre** (f)	stone
couvert	covered	**plan d'eau** (m)	lake
croisière (f)	cruise	**pleuvoir**	to rain
décoré	decorated	**pluie** (f)	rain
emplacement (m)	site, location, place, spot	**prise** (f)	electric point
en dehors de	outside	**privé**	private
ensoleillé	sunny	**prix** (m)	price, prize
entouré de	surrounded by	**propriétaire** (m)	owner
entrée (f)	entrance	**propriété** (f)	property
escalier (m)	staircase	**pêche** (f)	fishing
faible	weak	**rafale** (f)	gust of wind
fermé	closed	**renseignement** (m)	information
fleur (f)	flower	**rotin** (m)	cane for weaving
fort	strong	**réduit**	reduced
forteresse (f)	fortress	**siècle** (m)	century
gratuit	free	**soleil** (m)	sun
gîte (m)	self-catering holiday home	**spectacle** (m)	show
habité	lived in, inhabited	**tarif** (m)	price, cost
horaire (f)	timetable	**temps** (m)	weather
jouet (m)	toy	**terrain** (m)	ground
location (f)	hiring, renting	**vacancier** (m)	holiday maker
logement (m)	lodging, place to stay	**vannerie** (f)	basket work
lourd	heavy	**vent** (m)	wind
		verglas (m)	ice on roads

Acknowledgements

The authors would like to thank the following for their help and support:
Marie-Christine Perret, Sue Armour, Elaine Proffitt, Norman Silverstone, Ruth and
Stuart Bourne.

Photographs are reproduced by permission of:
Sally and Richard Greenhill p. 7
ZEFA p. 9 *all*, p. 19, p. 23 *all*, p. 28 *top*, p. 60, p. 90, p. 108, *a, e*
S.G.B. Brown p. 26
Norman Silverstone p. 28 *bottom*, p. 40 *top right, bottom left*, p. 72, p. 131
Jane Palmer p. 40 *top left*
Keith Nettle p. 40 *bottom right*, p. 67 *top right*
David Simson/DAS Photo p. 45, p. 51, p. 55 *bottom*, p. 67 *bottom left*, p. 80, p. 82, p. 108 *d*,
p. 110
Laurence Kimpton p. 55 *top*, p. 108 *b*
Keith Gibson p. 59, p. 66, p. 67 *top left, bottom right*, p. 70, p. 71, p. 75, p. 78, p. 97, p. 107,
p. 145, p. 148
French Government Tourist Office p. 108 *c*, p. 150 *Amboise, Chenonceau*
Mary Evans Picture Library p. 151

Other copyright material is reproduced by permission of:

L'Equipe p. 14; TOMY UK Ltd p. 24; French Railways (SNCF) pp. 110, 126; Auberge du
Beau Rivage p. 119 *left*; Michelin Tyre PLC (from the Michelin Red Guide 'France', 1990
edition) p. 119 *top right*; Office Municipal du Tourisme, Berck sur Mer pp. 119 *lower right*,
120; The Guardian p. 139; Crédit Agricole p. 140 *top right*; Chaussures Garanne p. 140
middle right; Framboisine p. 140 bottom; Colette Bouffault-Chabot p. 144; Office du
Tourisme de Blois p. 146; Compagnie de Navigation de la Loire p. 147; Gîtes de France
Ltd pp. 153, 154.

Every effort has been made to contact the copyright holders of material reproduced. The
publishers would be pleased to rectify omissions in future printings.